# Insight from the Eyes
## The Science of Effective Reading Instruction

Eric J. Paulson
and
Ann E. Freeman

Foreword by Kenneth S. Goodman

HEINEMANN
Portsmouth, NH

**Heinemann**
A division of Reed Elsevier Inc.
361 Hanover Street
Portsmouth, NH 03801–3912
www.heinemann.com

*Offices and agents throughout the world*

The authors and publisher wish to thank those who have generously given permission to reprint borrowed material:

Excerpts of "Wide O-" by Elsin Ann Graffam are reprinted with permission from *Ellery Queen's Mystery Magazine.* Copyright © 1968 by David Publications, Inc.

Excerpts from *Me Llamo Maria Isabel* by Alma Flor Ada and *My Name Is Maria Isabel* by Alma Flor Ada, translated from the Spanish by Ana M. Cerro, are reprinted with the permission of Atheneum Books for Young Readers, an imprint of Simon & Schuster Children's Publishing Division. Text Copyright © 1993 by Alma Flor Ada.

Excerpts of "Frugal Gourmets" by Annette Foglino are reprinted from *Civilization,* August/September 1998. Used by permission of the author.

Excerpts of "Waterford Ghost's Revenge" are reprinted with permission of Sterling Publishing Co., Inc. NY, NY. From *The Weirdest People in the World* by Carroll B. Colby. Copyright © 1973, 1965 by C. B. Colby.

Excerpt of "Review: Reading and Learning in Content Areas" by M. Rekrut in *Journal of Reading,* 38(5) is reprinted by permission of the International Reading Association. All rights reserved.

**Library of Congress Cataloging-in-Publication Data**
Paulson, Eric J.
   Insight from the eyes : the science of effective reading instruction /
Eric J. Paulson and Ann E. Freeman ; foreword by Kenneth S. Goodman.
       p. cm.
   Includes bibliographical references and index.
   ISBN 0-325-00582-6 (alk. paper)
   1. Reading.    2. Eye—Movements.    I. Freeman, Ann (Ann E.)    II. Title.

LB1050.P369 2003
372.41—dc21                                                    2003006680

Editor: Lois Bridges
Production: Vicki Kasabian
Cover design: Jenny Jensen Greenleaf
Typesetter: Argosy
Manufacturing: Jamie Carter

Printed in the United States of America on acid-free paper
07 06 05 04 03   DA   1 2 3 4 5

*This one's for Christina, Marina, and Alexandros.*

*~Eric*

*To my parents, David and Yvonne,*
*who have dedicated so many books to their daughters.*
*I happily dedicate this book to them.*

*~Ann*

# Contents

# Foreword

While their book is straightforward and easy to read, Eric Paulson and Ann Freeman have nevertheless given themselves a daunting task. They have set out to let their research on eye movements in reading help readers of this book—who may vary in their knowledge and views of what reading is and how it works—to achieve an understanding of the reading process quite at odds with prevalent commonsense views of reading. Furthermore, they go on to provide practical and useful ways of using the research insights of what readers do as they attempt to make sense of print to build curriculum and learning experiences for teachers of students with varying levels of proficiency.

They are remarkably successful in achieving their goals. The examples the authors provide from their research and that of others, both historical and contemporary, ring true because they are authentic. We are shown real readers reading from whole, real texts, not texts created for the purpose of research. The authors show the actual patterns of eye fixations, enabling us to see into what the eyes and brains of the readers are doing as they transact with the texts to construct meaning. The authors then show how these eye fixation patterns relate to oral miscue analysis of the same readings, which provides a deeper understanding of how perception is used in the construction of meaning.

Using these insights drawn from the authentic research examples, the authors go further, showing how they as teachers have used them to produce instructional experiences for their own students' developing literacy. While quite specific in that they build on the specific patterns those readers in their studies have shown, these instructional extensions can also illustrate ways that we can devise our own instructional applications.

In designing this book, the authors have chosen to present excerpts from the reading of stories by individual readers, showing details of the patterns of their eye movements and oral reading. They then help us to understand what they see in these patterns, presenting the rationale for their interpretations and explaining why they reject other interpretations. In doing the latter they deal with some common mis-representations and misinterpretations of eye movement research without setting up straw men. They quote liberally from other writers so as not to misrepresent their views. And they are careful to show how their data is consistent with the data of other eye movement researchers. They make clear that they differ with some conclusions about eye movement made by interpreters of past studies but not with the data of the researchers themselves.

A key misconception in the literature is that eye movement research has shown that readers attend to every letter of every word in a text in a quite linear, left-to-right way. They demonstrate that neither their research nor any other eye movement research supports such a conclusion.

In demonstrating this contradiction between the research and the common interpretations, they show that it is not the research but the underlying assumptions of the interpreters that have led to the unwarranted conclusions.

Some researchers like to say, "I only know what I see." To them Piaget was reported to have responded, "No, you only see what you know."

In their research and the way that they interpret other eye movement research, the authors go beyond their data, using what they know about the reading process to show what they see in the data. It is a circular process, in fact, in which what you know helps you to see which in turn refines what you know.

Wisely, I think, the authors wait until the last chapter to explicitly state what they know about the reading process and particularly the role of perception in reading and how that base of knowledge is at the same time rooted in insights from their research and used in understanding the patterns of eye movements and miscues their readers show. In this last chapter they demonstrate a view of research as developing explanations for underlying structures and processes rather than looking for simple cause-effect relationships. By waiting until this last chapter to explicate their theory the authors let the readers see how that theory is consistent with the patterns the readers have shown. And because the research deals with authentic literacy events—real readers reading real texts—it is easily applied to the classroom.

Much has been said in recent legislation about the need for educational practice to be rooted in scientific research. Too often, however, what is meant by "research" is statistical trials of instructional methods or materials with only gain scores on questionable tests offered as "scientific proof." With that reasoning what works is decided by gain scores. Teachers are not helped by understanding how to use such conclusions in their instruction and, in fact, are constrained from challenging the programs thus anointed as research based.

If science is to help teachers it must be real science that teachers can understand, learn from, and use as informed professionals. In this book, Paulson and Freeman treat their intended audience with respect. They say to us: "Here is what readers do as they read. Here is how we explain what they do and why we feel justified in rejecting other interpretations. And here is how we apply our knowledge in our teaching." Their advice is scientific, not because of experimental designs or significant data on test scores, but because it is based on theoretically sound analyses of the reality of reading. And informed professionals can confirm and accept or reject this advice with their own pupils in their own classrooms.

The authors have thus not only offered a very useful book for teachers. They have demonstrated in an important way how science could and should be applied in literacy instruction.

Kenneth S. Goodman
Professor Emeritus
Language, Reading and Culture
University of Arizona, Tucson

# Acknowledgments

We'd like to thank Eric's students—graduate students in literacy studies and adult/college developmental reading students—who consistently showed him what kind of research is necessary, pertinent, useful, and, yes, interesting. We'd also like to thank Ann's volunteer readers—bilingual graduate students and bilingual fourth-grade students—who took the time to read and discuss texts—readers who helped her answer so many questions and, of course, ask many, many more.

Thanks to our professors and teachers throughout the years who encouraged the thinking part of learning, especially Elizabeth Platt, Kathy Short, Luis Moll, Grant Brown, Fred Jenks, Jean Fennacy, and Debbie Manning.

Thanks especially to Ken and Yetta Goodman, for following up on mutual interests in discovering new ways to investigate the reading process.

To our colleagues who have bounced EMMA ideas around with us for years: Alan Flurkey, Andrea Garcia, Peter Duckett, Peter Fries, Vanessa Chacón, Koomi Kim, Joel Brown, Sapargul Mirseitova, and Jeanne Henry.

To the Support Crew, always ready to talk about another piece of the puzzle in some way or another: Michaeline Laine, John Bryan, Terry Bullock, Chet Laine, Janet Reed, Thomas Cook, and the incredible educators at the Hong Kong International School Lower Primary. Special thanks to our editor, Lois Bridges, and a big thank-you to our families.

# Introduction

## Why a Book on Eye Movements?

A few years ago, when reading a draft of an article about reading assessments, a colleague pointed to a spot in the text and said, "If I were reading this in a journal, I would have just stopped here." The spot she stopped at? The part of the article that began talking about eye movements.

After giving a conference presentation several years ago, an audience member came up to talk and said, "When you started talking about eye movements, I rolled my eyes and thought, 'Here we go again.'"

At a different conference, a group of attendees were having an informal, coffee-shop chat about literacy research when a well-meaning colleague earnestly asked, "Why would you want to do eye movement research? Don't you know the eye movement studies are wrong?"

These are not unusual reactions among reading educators—reactions, as we see it, caused by two main factors. The first is that much of the eye movement research from the 1950s, 1960s, and 1970s that has focused on "reading" has been done not by reading educators, but by psychologists whose definition of reading is somewhat different than many educators' definitions. Their experiments often had subjects looking at a single word or an out-of-context phrase or sentence. Either of these tasks, while fitting some definitions of reading, is at best an inauthentic, purposeless experience for the reader. Throughout this book, we provide examples of our own research that involve the reader reading authentic, complete texts with no task except to retell the story when finished.

The second reason many educators may be suspicious of eye movement research is that the results of much of the research have been misconstrued—and these faulty interpretations have been summarized and included in books and articles. Unfortunately, it is these summaries, not the research itself, that are cited. Because of this, eye movement research is widely misunderstood in some circles. Throughout this book, we point out misconceptions about eye movement research and attempt to correct those misconceptions through a look at the body of actual eye movement research, not simply summarizations of that research. Through reviews of eye movement literature, including our own studies and a mini-research project we will have you engage in, we hope to convey the idea that eye movement research supports a view of reading as a constructive, meaning-making process.

Still, we haven't really answered the question, why a book on eye movements? It comes down to this: the eyes represent what the reader is paying attention to on a millisecond-by-millisecond basis. We know what word the reader looked at, where the reader went next, if the reader skipped a word, went back to the previous sentence, looked at a word for a long time or a short time, and so on; in essence, eye movement recording produces a *map of the reader's reading process*. With this map, there is a great deal we can learn about how readers read. A major part of our purpose here is to discuss what eye movement research has revealed about the reading process. But we won't simply ask you to take our word for it. In addition to using many examples for illustrative purposes, we'll also provide an excerpt from an eye movement recording and encourage you to use this excerpt as a mini-research project throughout the book.

We are also concerned, however, with what happens *after* eye movement research. Therefore, we provide ideas for instruction that are based on what eye movement research demonstrates about reading. We should point out that none of the strategies we include are eye movement exercises (there was a misguided effort half a century ago to help poor readers read better by forcing their eyes to behave like the eyes of good readers—if this sounds like the tail wagging the dog, you're right, and these programs obviously didn't help anyone read better). We provide step-by-step directions for instructional strategies that are based on what eye movement research findings reveal about the reading process, and we also introduce a new strategy that uses a reader's own eye movement record as a teaching tool.

In the first chapter of the book we present a primer on eye movement basics, and we introduce and discuss the eye movements of Tim, a teenage reader. We use Tim's example throughout the book as an opportunity for you to do some mini-research. At the end of Chapter 1 are some questions about Tim's eye movement excerpt that correspond to the information in the primer.

The second, third, and fourth chapters all deal with discussions about new, recent, and classic eye movement research and what it tells us about the reading process and reading instruction. In addition to Tim's excerpt, we use examples from readers of different age groups throughout each chapter that illustrate each eye movement concept, and we encourage you to think about what each concept means in terms of teaching theory and practice. Questions are provided for individual or group use in extending and thinking further about the concepts discussed. At the end of each of these chapters, we describe strategies for reading instruction that are based on the principles of the eye movement research concepts in that chapter. Each instructional strategy includes a brief introduction, preparation tips, and step-by-step procedures for working through the strategy with students.

The fifth chapter describes a new instructional strategy that uses a reader's own eye movement record to improve his or her reading comprehension. We detail how this strategy worked with Tim.

The sixth chapter summarizes the findings we've presented throughout the book and discusses the links eye movement research makes to reading as a constructivist act.

You do *not* need an eye tracker to put into use the strategies found here, except for the one that is the subject of Chapter 5. But, even so, the days of eye movement labs being huge and expensive are over— eye trackers are small, unobtrusive, and many can be purchased for the same price as a commercial assessment package. In fact, while we're still a ways away from each reading teacher having her own eye tracker, there are already many public schools and school districts around the United States that own and use eye trackers.

So what is our purpose in writing this book? One important purpose is to illustrate and examine what eye movements reveal about the reading process. We do this by discussing the body of eye movement research, including our own studies. Instead of simply telling you what eye movement research has discovered, we also present many examples of eye movement records that we hope you will use as mini-research projects throughout the course of reading the book, so that you have the opportunity to discover salient eye movement findings yourself. Along the way, we also discuss misconceptions about eye movement research and what the corresponding truths are.

Another essential purpose of this book is to extrapolate instructional strategies from eye movement research. That is, we translate what eye movement research has shown us about the reading process into reading strategies teachers can implement with their students. We introduce and describe reading strategies for use with early readers, developing readers, content area literacy concerns, secondary reading, and college and adult reading. Many of these strategies are adaptable for a variety of reading levels and ages, and our hope is that the examples we give here will stimulate the creation of more strategies for use in your classrooms.

Whether you have occasion to use these strategies or not, our third major goal mirrors our belief that knowledge is an educator's greatest ally. Our hope is that *Insight from the Eyes* will increase your research-based understanding of how reading *works* and that it can play a part in your approach to reading education.

# Chapter 1

## A Look at Eye Movements

*A*s you begin to read this chapter, think about what the eyes do during reading. Are they flowing smoothly across the line, or do they stop and start? Do they always go in one direction, or do they go forward and backward? If you can, ask someone right now to read something while you watch his eyes. What do his eye movements look like?

By watching someone else's eyes as he reads, you've replicated one of the first eye movement studies ever, by French professor Emile Javal, in 1879. You've probably observed the same thing he did: that the reader's eyes don't flow continuously across a line of text but instead make a series of stops and starts. The stops are called fixations, and the movements between them are called saccades. It's not a smooth movement at all; in fact, the term *saccade* comes from the French word for "jerky movement," and that's what the eyes do as they move across the page: make a sequence of jerky stops and starts.

Shortly after Javal's observation, research was begun in order to find out why the eye makes fixations instead of simply scanning text. Researchers suspected it had something to do with whether the eyes could see while they were moving, so they structured early experiments around that question. For example, Dodge (1900) constructed an experiment to explore whether the eye picks up any information while it moves. He positioned two pieces of cardboard one behind the other and cut a slit into the center of the piece in front. Subjects, who sat in front of the cardboard pieces, were told to look first at a point to the left of the slit and then to make a single eye movement to a point to the right of the slit. The subjects couldn't see the slit itself when looking at either the right or the left fixation point. Dodge placed six different colors on the rear piece of cardboard five times

*1*

each to determine whether the subjects saw the color through the slit as they moved their eyes past it. Dodge reported that "when the eye movement was unbroken, the observer was unable to tell what had been exposed or even that anything at all had broken the black of the perimeter" (461). While their eyes were moving, the subjects couldn't tell that there was any change in color at all.

Dodge's study was one of the first to demonstrate that during a saccade—when the eye is in motion—no information is being sent to the brain. In other words, the only time the eye transmits usable data to the brain is when it stops, during a fixation; this basic finding has been replicated many times (see Wolverton and Zola 1983, for example). During saccades the movement is so fast that the eye doesn't see anything, not even a blur.

So the eye must fixate—come to a full stop—on something in order to see it; in terms of reading processes, this means that in order to see the letters in a word, that word must be fixated. So regardless of what some speed-reading infomercials would have you believe, you can't merely sweep your eyes over a page of print and see anything at all. That's not the only limitation the eye has as a data source, however; other *physiological* (not perceptual!) limitations involve *how much* text can be seen during one fixation. The eye has access to three regions of viewing information during a fixation: the foveal, parafoveal, and peripheral regions. The foveal region is the area that we think of as being in focus, and it extends about three to six letter spaces (one to two degrees of visual angle). The parafoveal region is adjacent to the foveal region, and the peripheral region includes everything in the visual field beyond the parafoveal region (Just and Carpenter 1987, 30). Figure 1–1 below illustrates the size of the foveal and parafoveal fields of vision.

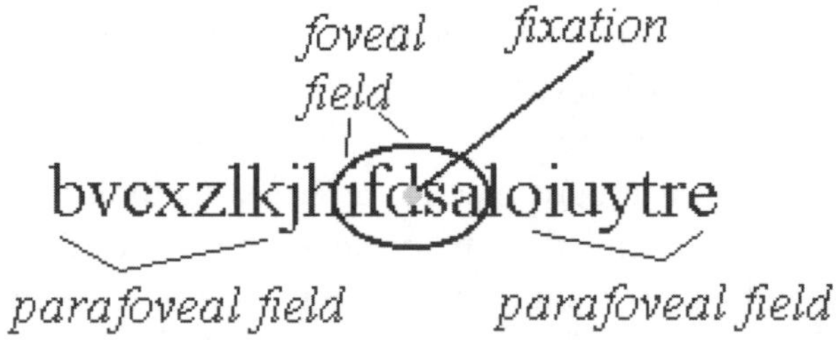

Figure 1–1

The farther away a letter is from the point of fixation and the small foveal field, the more difficult it is to identify (Rayner and Sereno 1994). When readers fixate a word, they have up to three or six letter spaces in focus, beyond which the print rapidly becomes fuzzy and out-of-focus. In fact, if you were presented with a random string of letters, you wouldn't be able to identify the letters that fell in the parafoveal and peripheral regions (but while reading meaningful text, you can "see" more, as we'll talk about soon!).

So, we know that eye movements during reading consist of a series of stops and starts, but it probably doesn't feel that way to you when you read. The process can be compared to viewing a traditional movie filmstrip, which, while actually constructed of still pictures (fixations), we perceive as a continuous whole.

Because Dodge's and other researchers' experiments indicated that no useful information is received during the movement of the eyes, those interested in reading processes decided research should concentrate on the pauses the eyes make. Simply watching someone read wasn't enough, of course, and it became necessary to devise a way to measure the exact location and duration of each fixation. Thus was born the first eye tracker.

## How Do Eye Trackers Work?

One of the earliest eye trackers involved an actual physical connection to the reader's eye. Huey (1908) reports of a method that involved a plaster of paris cup with a hole in the center, which was placed on the cornea of one eye, much as a contact lens. The cup was attached to an aluminum pointer that responded to the slightest eye movement. As a subject read, the pointer traced the movement of the eye on a piece of paper. Subsequent eye trackers were less intrusive; Buswell describes a method that is similar in theory to many eye-tracking methods still used today. By photographing a beam of light reflected first to a subject's cornea from silvered glass mirrors, and then from the cornea through a camera lens to moving kinetoscope film, researchers could record the changing positions of the beam of light on film, which provided an "accurate record showing the position and duration of each fixation of the eye while the subject [read]" (Buswell 1922, 12).

These early eye trackers were large and unwieldy, however, and surely would have seemed intimidating to the readers. The advent of the microcomputer in the 1970s brought more accurate and smaller eye trackers into play, but they were still daunting and intrusive to some extent—for example, readers' heads were locked in place through the use of chin rests, headrests, bite bars, and more, so they could move only their eyes.

As the technology advanced, eye trackers began to use head-mounted optics, so readers could move their heads normally as they read. While some of these units were heavy and awkward, others were less intrusive. Eventually, remote eye trackers that could correct for head movements were developed, and with these systems nothing needs to touch the reader. These eye trackers bounce an infrared beam of light off the reader's eye, which allows the computer to record eye position by measuring pupil and corneal reflections. All the eye movement examples you'll see here were recorded with Applied Science Laboratories Model 504 Eye Trackers, an unobtrusive remote eye tracker, at the University of Arizona and the University of Cincinnati. The photo in Figure 1–2 shows a young reader in front of the ASL 504 Eye Tracker. The eye-

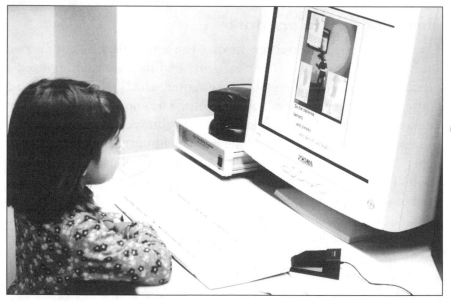

Figure 1–2

tracking camera is in front and to the left of the reader; it's the black object one reader described as a "fancy electric pencil sharpener." Around the lens of the camera are light sources that reflect harmless, invisible infrared light off the pupil and front surface of the cornea and send that signal back to the eye-tracking processor (the white box just visible to the left of the computer monitor) and then to the eye-tracking computer, which can measure exactly where on a page of text a reader is looking, and for how long she looked there. The eye-tracking data are viewed in two basic ways. One is in a still-image over-lay of fixations on top of the text the reader read, which is illustrated in Figure 1–3. The other is through a real-time video of the text that is being read, with a small cursor that represents the reader's eyes moving along the text as she reads. This type of data can be recorded using a normal videotape recorder. A small multidirectional microphone sits out of sight and captures the reader's oral reading, which is recorded simultaneously on the same VHS tape as the real-time eye movement data. Thus we are able to see where the reader looked while listening to what the reader read, a powerful type of data that we will explore using as a reading instructional strategy in Chapter 5.

A word about procedures: We believe that eye trackers can be to eye movements what tape recorders are to oral speech—an unobtrusive recording of language processes. To this end, we strive to help our readers be as comfortable as possible while reading in front of the eye tracker. We demonstrate how the eye tracker works by trying it out on ourselves or on a lab assistant. Before they begin reading, we explain the system to them and encourage them to ask any questions they would like about how it "tape-records the eyes." They then read some practice texts to get comfortable. During the eye-tracking session, the readers' only task is to read, either aloud or silently. The texts they read are all complete, authentic texts, and after they read, they retell the text any way they like, as a measure of comprehension. These pro-cedures help us work toward making the eye-tracking experience as authentic a reading experience as possible.

## What Does an Eye Movement Record Look Like?

Let's take a look at what a reader's eye movements look like, when superimposed on the text he read. This reader is Tim, a self-described insecure reader in his late teens. We'll come back to Tim's example throughout the book, including, in later chapters, a look at his oral reading and an in-depth look at an instructional strategy used with Tim. In this excerpt of the short story "Wide O-" (the entire story is provided in the appendix and a full-size copy is downloadable at www. heinemann.com/paulsonfreeman), the dots indicate fixations, and the lines between them indicate movement from one fixation to the next (see Figure 1–3). (A larger version is available at www.heinemann.com/ paulsonfreeman.)

All the doors are locked, right? And all the windows, ditto. Okay, then. So I feel like an idiot, trying to stay up all night. Well, sitting here in the living room is a lot better than doing what I did the last time Bill was away overnight! Locking myself in the bathroom and staying there until dawn, for heaven's sake- Oh . Oh, the furnace clicked on, that's all that was! Calm down, girl, calm down! The trouble with you is, you read the papers. You should read the comies and stop there.

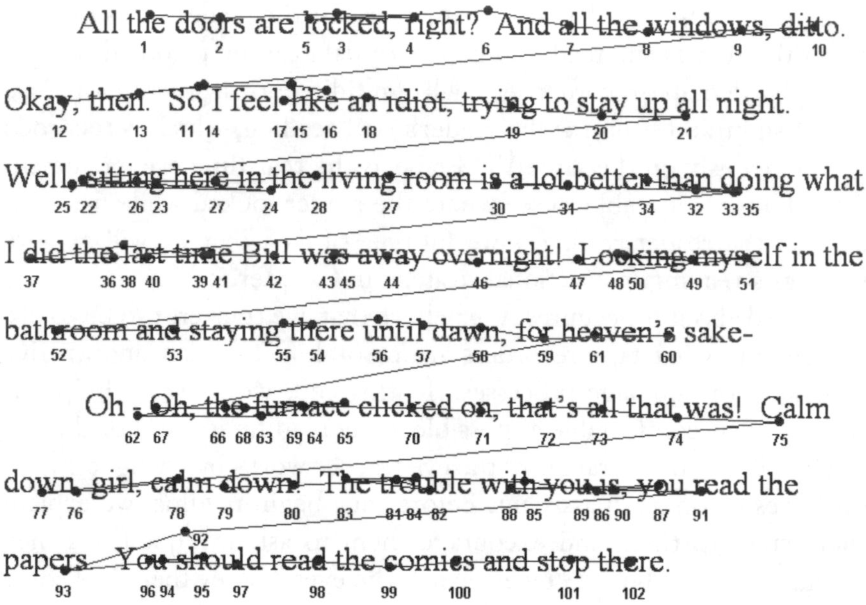

Figure 1–3

The first fixation on the first line is on *the*, followed by a fixation on *doors*, a fixation on *locked*, then on *right*, then back to *locked*, before moving on to the next sentence. Note that not every word is looked at, and not every fixation goes left to right. We also want to examine how long Tim looked at each word; the chart below provides the duration, in milliseconds, of each of the fixations he made:

| Fixation Number | Fixation Duration | Fixation Number | Fixation Duration | Fixation Number | Fixation Duration | Fixation Number | Fixation Duration | Fixation Number | Fixation Duration | Fixation Number | Fixation Duration | Fixation Number | Fixation Duration |
|---|---|---|---|---|---|---|---|---|---|---|---|---|---|
| 1 | 467 | 22 | 617 | 43 | 317 | 64 | 250 | 85 | 533 | | | | |
| 2 | 383 | 23 | 233 | 44 | 683 | 65 | 283 | 86 | 250 | | | | |
| 3 | 300 | 24 | 500 | 45 | 200 | 66 | 567 | 87 | 167 | | | | |
| 4 | 300 | 25 | 500 | 46 | 800 | 67 | 917 | 88 | 383 | | | | |
| 5 | 333 | 26 | 317 | 47 | 167 | 68 | 350 | 89 | 350 | | | | |
| 6 | 200 | 27 | 683 | 48 | 283 | 69 | 883 | 90 | 500 | | | | |
| 7 | 300 | 28 | 400 | 49 | 283 | 70 | 683 | 91 | 800 | | | | |
| 8 | 567 | 29 | 217 | 50 | 217 | 71 | 383 | 92 | 100 | | | | |
| 9 | 1,083 | 30 | 683 | 51 | 283 | 72 | 833 | 93 | 500 | | | | |
| 10 | 167 | 31 | 350 | 52 | 383 | 73 | 567 | 94 | 950 | | | | |
| 11 | 117 | 32 | 333 | 53 | 367 | 74 | 1,283 | 95 | 233 | | | | |
| 12 | 450 | 33 | 150 | 54 | 567 | 75 | 317 | 96 | 267 | | | | |
| 13 | 483 | 34 | 267 | 55 | 367 | 76 | 267 | 97 | 383 | | | | |
| 14 | 467 | 35 | 183 | 56 | 267 | 77 | 150 | 98 | 233 | | | | |
| 15 | 550 | 36 | 183 | 57 | 233 | 78 | 267 | 99 | 733 | | | | |
| 16 | 700 | 37 | 367 | 58 | 367 | 79 | 767 | 100 | 217 | | | | |
| 17 | 267 | 38 | 250 | 59 | 483 | 80 | 217 | 101 | 483 | | | | |
| 18 | 550 | 39 | 400 | 60 | 700 | 81 | 333 | 102 | 250 | | | | |
| 19 | 567 | 40 | 300 | 61 | 117 | 82 | 117 | | | | | | |
| 20 | 383 | 41 | 500 | 62 | 500 | 83 | 300 | | | | | | |
| 21 | 300 | 42 | 733 | 63 | 300 | 84 | 117 | | | | | | |

Between the fixation overlay in Figure 1–3 and the above chart of Tim's durations, we have a considerable amount of information. So much information, in fact, that there is often a reluctance to look closely at the data, because it seems overwhelming. We know where Tim looked; for how long; whether he looked at a word once, twice, or more; whether he went backward, skipped a word, regressed to a word he skipped, regressed to refixate a word he already examined; and so on. By examining his record, we have a map of his reading.

Let's think about this map as the pioneers of eye movement research did. To bring us back to the first part of the chapter, after Javal observed readers stopping throughout a text, Dodge, Huey, Buswell, and other researchers began to center their questions around *where* the reader fixates, for *how long*, and *why*. Let's think about Tim's fixations in the same way: where, when, and why did Tim fixate where he did? We invite you to use this example to conduct some eye movement research of your own:

1. Is every word fixated? _____

   How many words are fixated? _____

   There are ninety-four words in this excerpt. What is the percentage of fixated words? _____

2. Is every word fixated for the same amount of time? _____

   What is the shortest fixation? _____ The longest? _____

3. Do all the fixations go in the same direction—left to right, word-by-word? _____

   How many fixations go in a different direction? _____

4. Does the choice of which word is fixated seem arbitrary? _____

   Are all the fixated words the same part of speech? _____

   Number of nouns fixated _____

   Number of verbs fixated _____

   Number of adjectives fixated _____

   Number of adverbs fixated _____

   Number of pronouns fixated _____

   Number of prepositions fixated _____

   Number of articles fixated _____

   Number of conjunctions fixated _____

Over the next few chapters, we'll refer back to this example several times as we progress through what is generally understood—and misunderstood—about what eye movements reveal about the reading process.

## Summary

Much of this chapter has been concerned with setting the stage for a discussion of eye movements. Information about how the eyes transmit information, knowledge of how eye trackers work, and an understanding of the kind of data that eye movement recording produces are all prerequisites for understanding what eye movements can show us about reading. To that end, we introduced an eye movement excerpt from Tim, our teenage reader, and encouraged you to look at different aspects of his eye movements. Over the next few chapters, we'll come back to Tim's excerpt again to make different points about reading, and in Chapter 5 we'll show how Tim responds to a new instructional strategy using his own eye movements.

# Chapter 2

## How Many Words Do Readers Look At?

One reason that Javal's observation about readers' eyes making frequent stops and starts is interesting is that it is counterintuitive—most of us are not aware of our eyes' movements at all, much less that they stop and start three or four times a second. Throughout this book, we'll examine some other intuitions readers hold. In this chapter, we want to think about the number of words that readers fixate, or look at, while reading. Think about your own reading experiences—does it feel as if you see every letter and every word on the page? Probably! But there is a crucial difference between your *perception* of what you see and what your eyes actually look at—fixate— as we'll discuss here.

If you've taken a close look at Tim's excerpt in the previous chapter, you've noticed that although he makes a lot of fixations, he doesn't look at all the words. A good example of this is in the first two lines of that excerpt, shown below (Figure 2–1):

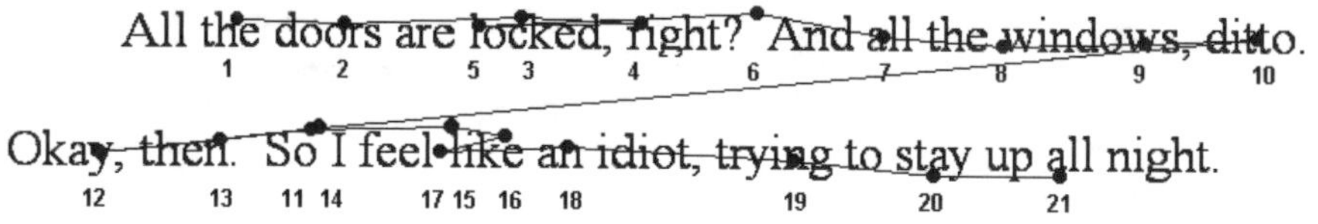

All the doors are locked, right? And all the windows, ditto.
   1     2      5  3     4      6      7     8     9    10

Okay, then. So I feel like an idiot, trying to stay up all night.
 12     13   11 14    17 15 16  18      19    20    21

Figure 2–1

In fact, he doesn't even come close. In this excerpt, about 60 percent of the words are fixated; over the entire story, he looked at around 72 percent of the words. So a bit less than one-third of all the words were

not looked at; this probably seems counterintuitive. Print is a necessary part of the reading experience, and it's difficult to understand how
a reader could skip a third of the words in a text and still have read it.
In fact, the feeling that we must look at each word is so strong that
some reading educators have furthered that assumption. For example,
Grossen states that "recent eye movement research indicates that
good readers do not sample the text and predict to recognize words
efficiently, but rather see every single letter on the page" (1997, 10).
Similarly, Liberman and Liberman express their view that "the elegant
studies of eye movements during reading by Rayner and his associates
have shown conclusively that good readers read every word" (1992,
352). So do we believe what Tim has shown us, or what reading
experts have told us that eye movements demonstrate?

Fortunately, we have more than a century of eye movement
research to refer to in answering this question. This research demonstrates that if anything, Tim fixates a few words *more* than the average
reader. For example, in looking at early research by eye movement
pioneer Buswell, Fisher and Shebilske found that "less than two-thirds
of the words were fixated in eight of the records and no more than
three-fourths in any of those remaining" (1985, 149). In Just and
Carpenter's 1987 study, 68 percent of the words were fixated (37), and
Hogaboam reports that in his study "about 40 percent of the words
were skipped" (315). Interestingly, Rayner, the very researcher that
Liberman and Liberman mention in their quote above as showing that
readers read every word, states in his review of eye movement literature that "at least 20 percent to 30 percent of the words in text are
skipped altogether (i.e. do not receive a fixation)" (1997, 319).

So there's a discrepancy there, but it comes down to what theorists
think *must* be the case with eye movements versus what eye movement
research shows *actually* happens. In short, readers skip 20 percent to 40
percent, or more, of the words in a text.

However, many eye movement studies examine college-age readers,
and the reader introduced in our tutorial example in Chapter 1, Tim,
is a teenage reader, so what about young readers? Do they also skip
words when reading, or do they look at every word?

The following excerpt (Figure 2–2) shows the eye movements of a
fourth-grade reader (Freeman 2001).

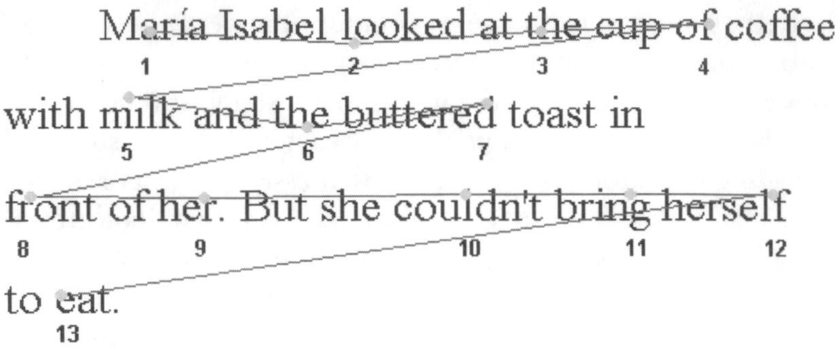

Maria Isabel looked at the cup of coffee
1        2        3        4

with milk and the buttered toast in
5       6       7

front of her. But she couldn't bring herself
8      9       10      11      12

to eat.
13

Figure 2–2

Here, the reader fixated thirteen out of the twenty-four words in this excerpt, or 54 percent. In her 2001 study, Freeman's fourth-grade bilingual readers fixated a similar amount, 56 percent of the words in the English texts they read. And there is evidence that even younger readers do not fixate every word. Duckett (2002) looked at the eye movements of first-grade readers, who fixated, on average, 80 percent of the words in the texts they read.

So, the younger the reader (more appropriately, the less literacy experience the reader has), the more fixations the reader makes during reading—but still without fixating every word. So far, we've discussed only English texts, though; could the phenomenon of reading without looking at every word be an artifact of the language or writing system? Freeman (2001) found that her fourth-grade bilingual readers fixated a similar percentage of words whether reading Spanish or English. In addition, different alphabetic systems do not seem to change the fact that reading doesn't require fixating on every word; the example below (Figure 2–3) is from the eye movement record of Sasha, a fourteen-year-old Russian student reading in her native language (Mirseitova and Paulson 2000).

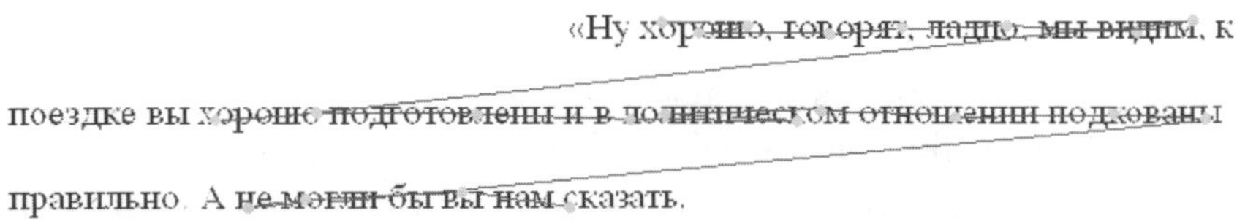

«Ну хорошо, говорят, ладно, мы видим, к

поездке вы хорошо подготовлены и в политическом отношении подкованы

правильно. А не могли бы вы нам сказать.

Figure 2–3

As you can see, she fixates about 53 percent of the words in the sentence excerpted here (the beginning of the second sentence is included to show where her first eye movements on the second line took place, as she didn't fixate the last word of the first sentence). Readers of non-alphabetic writing systems, like Chinese, also exhibit similar eye movement patterns (Sun, Morita, and Stark 1985).

These studies suggest that, regardless of age or language, reading doesn't seem to be dependent on looking at every single word. But that suggestion raises an interesting question: how can reading work if the reader doesn't have to look at each word?

To answer that question, the distinction of physiological data versus perceptual data needs to be made. In Chapter 1 we discussed the amount of in-focus information that is available to the reader around the point of fixation—as much as three to six letter spaces. This is a physiological measurement; that is, our example showed three to six letter spaces as being a string of random letters, as illustrated in Figure 2–4 below:

bvcxzlkjhifdsaloiuytre

Figure 2–4

When dealing with authentic text, of course, it's usually not strings of random letters one is faced with, although that doesn't change the amount of text that is in foveal focus. For example, in the sentence below (Figure 2–5), the same number of letter spaces are still in foveal focus, even though it's a sentence, not random letters:

Peter opened his eyes.

Figure 2–5

However, reading authentic, comprehensible text does change how much we *perceive*. As Frank Smith says, the more information we have behind the eyes, the less we need in front of the eyes (1994, 66–67).

The "Peter opened his eyes" excerpt is from a classic eye movement study done by Buswell in 1922, which we have been using in presentations for years. Figure 2–6 shows the complete excerpt Buswell provides of a college reader. In the sentence "Peter opened his eyes," the reader fixated only PETER and OPENED, yet she read and understood the entire sentence. How? The answer involves how readers use context as they construct meaning. By the time this reader arrived at "Peter opened," she had already read that the character Peter had gone to bed and was lying there when he heard a noise. After reading "Peter opened," the reader strongly predicted that it would be *his eyes* that Peter would be opening, and the fuzzy, out-of-focus print in the reader's parafoveal field was enough to confirm that prediction. Think of this as a very fast, almost subconscious cloze activity. As we'll discuss in the strategy sections at the end of this chapter, cloze activities involve the reader filling in blanks in a text based on the information preceding the blank and the reader's predictions.

Figure 2–6

Another way to view this phenomenon of nonfixated words being perceived is to think of what readers are able to see in one glance as the *perceptual span*. For English texts, readers are able to perceive more to the right of the point of fixation than they are to the left of the point of fixation, and for readers of Hebrew texts, which are printed from right to left, there is more information gained to the left of the point of fixation (Rayner and Pollatsek 1989). That is, we see more text in the direction we are reading, almost as if we were looking ahead of ourselves to see where the text is going. This perception of text to the right of the point of fixation can be as large as fourteen or fifteen letter spaces, while we perceive only three or four letter spaces to the left of fixation (Rayner 1995, 7). It is important to understand that the perceptual span is larger than the foveal region of focus *when reading connected text*. When reading random letter strings, or even text that is very difficult for the reader to comprehend, the perceptual span is reduced down to what we can think of as the physiological span—three to six letter spaces. In other words, the more comprehensible a text is to a reader, the more that reader is able to see at a single glance.

How does the perceptual span relate to the foveal field that we introduced in Chapter 1? It's useful to think of the foveal field of vision as *physiological*—what is actually in focus. The perceptual span, however, is what *we think we see*; places outside of the foveal region that seem in focus appear that way because our minds are able to fill in the blanks.

The idea that it is the reader's responsibility to fill in the blanks, to *make sense of* the information the eye presents to the reader, is an important one. Eye movement research provides evidence that a view of reading as simply a process of gaining letter-by-letter information, without reader perceptions entering the equation, doesn't hold much explanatory power. In fact, the foveal information the brain receives from the eyes is initially gibberish. For an illustration of how much in-focus graphic data is available when reading, we have spelled out what the eyes delivered to Tim while he read the excerpt in Figure 2–7. In other words, the text information available to readers based solely on foveal, in-focus information is nonsensical by itself.

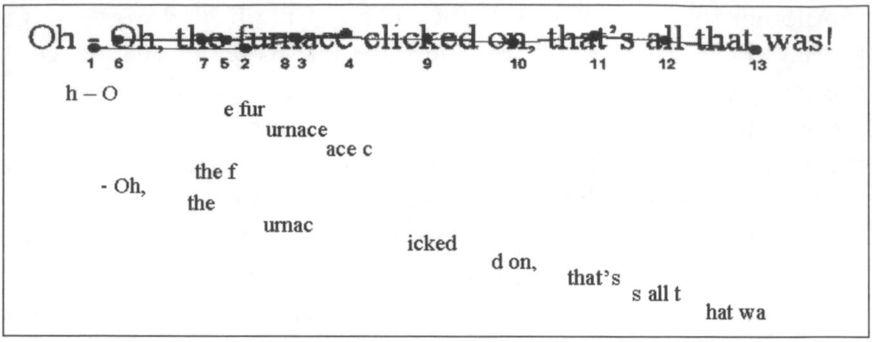

Oh - Oh, the furnace clicked on, that's all that was!
1 6 7 5 2 8 3 4 9 10 11 12 13
h – O
e fur
urnace
ace c
the f
- Oh,
the
urnac
icked
d on,
that's
s all t
hat wa

Figure 2–7

Figure 2–7 shows what Tim saw in the foveal field of vision while reading that line—what his eyes delivered to his brain in focus. Of course, he didn't see the text this way, for it would have been incomprehensible; instead, his brain took the available information and pieced it together into a seamless whole. In this perspective, *reading depends less on what the reader sees than on what the reader does with that information.*

However, the reader is not passively sitting back and trying to cope with random information; quite the opposite, the reader actively sends his eyes to places in the text where he wants and needs more information. One strong piece of evidence that supports the notion of an active reader is the type of words that readers tend to look at. In Chapter 1, we encouraged you to think about what type of words Tim fixated; you may have noticed that nouns and verbs received more fixations than articles and prepositions. This is also evident in the figure below, an excerpt from fourth grader Angel's reading (Freeman 2001):

Her knee hurt a lot, but María Isabel
1 2 3 4
was determined to walk to the bus without
5 6 7
stopping to look at it.
8 9

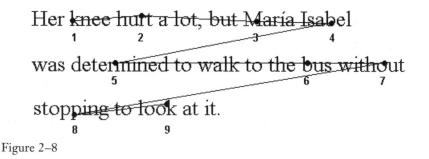

Figure 2–8

Only one of the words Angel fixates, the preposition *without*, is a function word, which has a largely grammatical role. The rest of his fixations land on words that carry more of the meaning of the sentence, termed content words. It makes sense; a reader actively searching for meaning shouldn't feel the need to thoroughly examine each function word in the text. In fact, that would be inefficient, when it's the content words that provide access to the author's intended meaning. If that is the case, we should see more content words fixated than function words, and this is borne out in Tim's example from Chapter 1, where he fixates around 80 percent of the content words in the text, compared with 54 percent of the function words. Other eye movement studies provide similar findings; for example, Just and Carpenter (1987) found that readers fixated approximately 38 percent of the function words and 83 percent of the content words in their study.

You may have noticed, however, that many content words are longer than function words. Does this mean that readers are simply looking at the biggest words in the sentence, and—luckily—these words carry meaning? The question of whether a word is skipped because of its length or a syntactic feature of the word was tested by O'Regan (1979). He recorded the eye movements of subjects who read pairs of sentences that began the same but ended differently (each subject read one sentence from each pair):

> *The dog that growled the most was friendly.*
> OR
> *The dog that growled ate many biscuits.*

> *He claimed the ladies the maid knew lived in New York.*
> OR
> *He claimed the ladies met many times to discuss.*

In these sentences readers skipped *the* substantially more than they skipped three-letter verbs. So in the first example given, *the* was more likely to be skipped in the first sentence than *ate* in the second sentence, and in the second example, the second *the* in the first sentence was more likely to be skipped than *met* in the second sentence, even though they're all three-letter words. O'Regan summarizes by stating that fixations "are controlled sufficiently rapidly to be influenced from moment to moment by information concerning the lexical category of a word in peripheral vision" (59). In other words, it's not chance or luck that guides a reader's eye movements, but an efficient process of looking for the most informative aspects of the text.

To round out some of our discussions here, let's replicate, in a way, an experiment that has been done with junior high– and college-age readers using a text written by Ken Goodman. Here are the instructions for you to try right now (you'll need a piece of paper and pen or pencil):

1. Read the following paragraph through one time.
2. After you have read it, cover the paragraph and write exactly what you remember reading.

### The Boat in the Basement

A woman was building a boat in her
basement. When she had finished the
the boot, she discovered that it was
too big to go though the door. So he
had to take the boat a part to get
it out. She should of planned ahead.

Compare what you wrote with the original. Any differences? Did you notice anything strange about the original—anything that seemed out of place? You may have noticed an inconsistency in the paragraph, something that's not quite right, an error. Didn't notice anything suspicious? Congratulate yourself for being a meaning-focused reader! Go back and look at the original again—how many errors are there in the paragraph?

Altogether there are six errors deliberately embedded in the paragraph: two *the*s, *boot* for *boat*, *though* for *through*, *he* for *she*, *a part* for *apart*, and *should of* for *should have* (or *should've*). For a description of a formal research project utilizing this paragraph, see Gollasch (1980), and for a more thorough description of the reading processes involved in reading this paragraph, see Goodman (1996). Xu (1998) reports on the parallel effect a Chinese translation of this paragraph has on Chinese readers. Similar trick paragraphs and phrases have been used for years by psychology teachers to help their students think about perceptual issues. For example, students would read the following phrases one time and write what they remembered reading:

PARIS
IN THE
THE SPRING

CAUTION
MEN AT
AT WORK

When asked to rewrite these phrases exactly as they see them, many readers omit the second *the* or *at*. It is as if the brain excludes information it doesn't need.

Phenomena such as these are generally used as an indication of the perceptual processes that occur during reading. What these projects and discussions have not touched upon is where the reader is looking while reading—and detecting errors in—the "Boat in the Basement" paragraph. Figure 2–9 shows the eye movements of Evan, a teenage reader, while reading and looking for errors in that paragraph. Evan was given the same instructions that we gave earlier: to read the paragraph one time through and write what he remembered reading. The points in Figure 2–9 indicate where Evan looked the first time he read the paragraph. His rate of words fixated is well within expected limits; he fixated about 61 percent of the words. In terms of the embedded

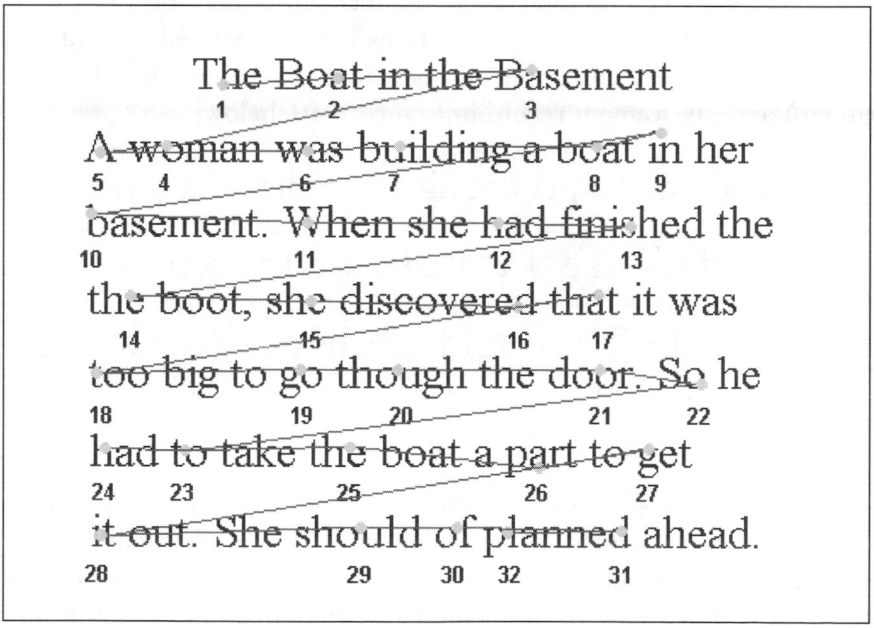

Figure 2–9

errors, he fixated one of the THEs, THOUGH, PART (from *a part*), and SHOULD OF. After reading it through one time, he wrote the following:

### The boat in the basement

A woman was building a boat in the basement. When she was through, she realized that it wouldn't fit through the door. The woman had to take it apart to fit it through the door. She should have planned better.

Note that while he fixated at least part of each of the errors mentioned above (*the*, *though*, *a part*, and *should of*), he used them—and spelled them—all correctly in his paragraph.

When he finished writing his version of the paragraph, he was asked if there seemed to be anything out of place. He said yes, something seemed weird, but he couldn't put his finger on it. He was told to look again, this time with unlimited time, to find what was out of place. He quickly found *he*, *boot*, and the two *the*s but didn't find the other three errors until they were pointed out to him. This is not at all uncommon; most people do not find all six errors, including the authors of this book when we first tried this paragraph. But it is interesting to look at some of Evan's fixations during his second reading of the paragraph. Since he was given unlimited time to read the paragraph the second time around, there were many fixations that overlapped. In order to present a relatively clean view of his reading, we've excerpted part of the total eye movement record in Figure 2–10, below:

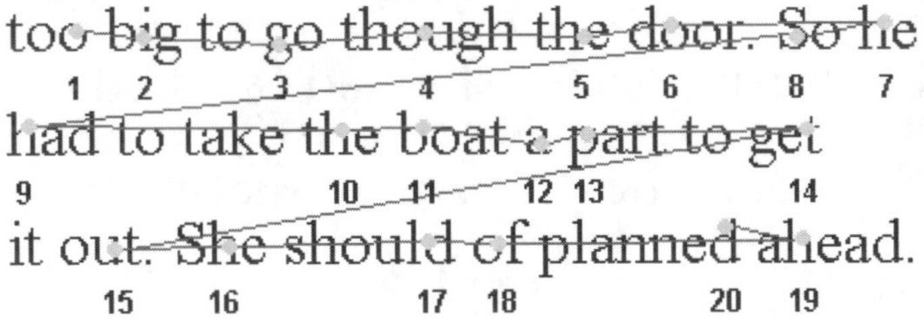

Figure 2–10

Notice that in this excerpt, Evan fixates THOUGH, A PART, and SHOULD OF—the three errors that he never detected. One might want to argue that since he looked at them, and didn't identify them as errors, he must not know how to spell them or use them in a sentence. But look again at his version of the paragraph that he wrote; he uses the word *through* three times, all correctly. He also spells and uses *apart* and *should have* correctly. Thus, all three undetected errors were not only looked at while reading the paragraph but also used correctly in his written version of the paragraph.

Evan shows us a reader who knows how to spell and use the word *through*; in fact, he uses the word three times in his written version of the "Boat in the Basement." While reading the "Boat" paragraph the first time, he fixated *though*, and then while reading the paragraph the second time, while searching for errors, he fixated *though* again, but he never identified the word as an error. Evan is a great example of a reader so focused on meaning that even while he's looking for errors, he "sees" the correct spelling.

Here again is a demonstration of the crucial difference between reading as direct input from printed page to brain and reading as a perceptual act. Evan's expectation of the word *through* was so strong that even while looking for anomalies he still perceived *through* instead of what was actually in the text. In the sentence "Peter opened his eyes" at the beginning of this chapter, Buswell's reader predicted the word *eyes* so strongly that she didn't even need to look at the word. Evan's excerpt shows the same strength in prediction in a slightly different way: Evan predicted the word *through* so strongly that even though he looked right at the text item *though* he still saw it as *through*. We'll talk more about that phenomenon in Chapter 4.

## Summary

In this chapter we discussed one of the most counterintuitive aspects of how the eyes work in reading: the fact that we don't look at every word when reading. Reader knowledge and print experience play an extremely important role in reading, which highlights the importance of context and prediction as elements of the reading process. We saw that even while searching for errors in a paragraph, readers can look directly at an error and not see it. We also pointed out that the eyes deliver incomplete information to the brain. Understanding this provides an important step in realizing that reading is a meaning-making act, a dialogue between author and reader.

The following questions will help you reflect on what you have learned from reading this chapter. We encourage you to work through the questions individually or in small groups. At the end of this chapter you will find instructional links to the eye movement concepts we have explored in this chapter. In this section, we present a variety of strategies that are supported by the eye movement research we have presented. These strategies can be used with your own students to help them explore the reading process and become more proficient in their reading.

## Extension Questions

1. The difference between what you see (physiologically) and what you think you see (perceptually) was raised and discussed in this chapter. Why is this distinction significant in understanding how readers read?

2. Several of our examples have demonstrated that readers from different language backgrounds have similar eye movement patterns, relative to the text they are reading. That is, regardless of whether the text is read from right to left, left to right, or top to bottom, readers still skip a similar percentage of words, still make regressions, and so on. Does this evidence provide support for the idea that there is a universal reading process? Or is it more likely that a Russian reader reads Russian radically differently than a Spanish reader reads Spanish?

3. From the evidence presented in this chapter, it is clear that readers do not look at anywhere near every word in a given text. How, then, does reading happen if readers don't have to look at each word?

4. As shown in the example in Figure 2–7, the actual print data that the eye delivers in focus to the brain is a seemingly incomprehensible graphic mess. Yet we still are able to comprehend what we read. How is this possible?

5. Readers fixate content words roughly twice as often as they fixate function words. This makes sense, as the content words carry much of the meaning of the sentence, while function words have a more grammatical role. But how do readers know that a content word is coming up, so they should fixate it, or that a function word is coming up, so they should skip it—without having to look at it to see?

6. The "Boat in the Basement" paragraph is a good example of how readers see what they expect to see. Eric uses similar texts with his graduate students; one example is from a Doonesbury cartoon, where a bartender asks a customer, "What can I do you for?" Most readers reading that aloud say instead, "What can I do for you?" which is the more expected phrasing of that question. Can you find other examples of this phenomenon in everyday print?

## Eye Movement Links to Reading Instruction

The "Boat in the Basement" activity described in this chapter is one strategy that can be used to help readers recognize that reading is not a process of word-by-word recognition but rather a process involving prediction and sampling of text. While trick paragraphs with these kinds of intentional errors are a great illustration of that process, even more powerful is the eye movement research that clearly shows readers *never* look at every word in a text. Why? Not because they can't but because they don't *need to* in order to read. And since the brain is concerned with efficiency, it's not about to direct the eyes to look at every word when it's getting the information it needs by actively sampling the text.

So when teachers and students downplay this natural process of prediction and attention to context, it can hinder, not help, a reader. One way to remind readers of the importance of paying attention to context is through cloze procedure activities.

### Cloze Procedure

In a cloze procedure, certain words are eliminated from a text. Readers are encouraged to focus on their predictions rather than solely on visual information in order to make sense of what they are reading. Beginning readers sometimes have difficulty making sense of stories if they are asked to focus in on every word of the text. Likewise, older readers often find reading difficult or new text even harder to make sense of when they focus too much on individual words; Frank Smith (1994, 80) calls this "tunnel vision," when readers focus so much on letter-level cues that they lose sight of the meaning of the sentence or even the phrase. In the following sections we describe two forms of cloze that can be done with different age groups: big book cloze with young readers and cloze with older readers.

For both groups, begin by discussing the following sample of text (Figure 2–11), which shows fourth grader Juan Antonio's fixations as he reads. It is helpful to make an overhead of this sample. Explain that the dots show where Juan Antonio looked as he read and that the numbers indicate the order of these fixations. Tell the students that Juan Antonio did not make any miscues when he read this page aloud. Use the questions listed below to guide your initial discussion. (A full-size reproducible can be found at www.heinemann.com/paulsonfreeman.)

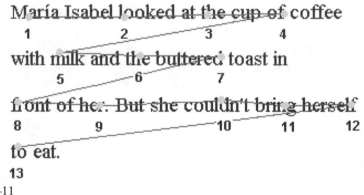

Figure 2–11

## Discussion Questions

- Did Juan Antonio look at every word as he read?
- How did Juan Antonio know what the words were if he didn't look at all of them?
- Do you think that good readers look at every word when they read?
- Do you think that you look at every word when you read?
- Do you think it's possible to get information from a story without looking at every word?

*Big Book Cloze During Shared Reading*

This strategy helps groups of young readers explore prediction in reading.

**Preparation:**   Select a big book with a predictable pattern. Read through the text and identify the first two times the pattern occurs. Place sticky notes over one or two of the words on each of the remaining pages. Try to select key words that make up the pattern found throughout the book. You may wish to cover the same word several times or select different words in the pattern. A text may end up looking something like this:

My teddy bear likes to eat with me.

My teddy ＿＿＿＿＿＿ likes to play with me.

My teddy bear ＿＿＿＿＿＿ to swim with me.

My teddy ＿＿＿＿＿＿ likes to ＿＿＿＿＿＿ with me.

**Procedure:**   After discussing Juan Antonio's reading, invite the children to sit together on the floor in an area in front of you so that they can all see the big book. Explain that some of the words in the book you will be reading together are covered up and that together you will see what happens during the reading.

Invite the students to chorally read the big book. Once the students have read a page that contains covered-up words, ask for volunteers to explain how they knew what the word was even if they could not see it. Continue to read through the text with the students. As appropriate, stop to have students discuss the strategies they used to figure out the covered-up words.

Once the students have done several big book cloze shared readings with pattern books, one alternative is to follow the same procedure with stories that do not exhibit regular patterns. Discuss whether the covered-up words in these stories were more or less difficult to predict. It is interesting to have students come up with a list of words that would work in place of the covered word before uncovering it to see what word the author chose to use.

*Cloze with Older Readers*

Older readers can work individually or in small groups to explore the use of prediction in reading.

**Preparation:** Once readers are older, cloze strategy can be presented on sheets of paper rather than as a shared reading. Instructors can photocopy a page of text with various words covered up or write a short story with some blank slots. Randomly select words to omit throughout the text or create a systematic cloze. One way to prepare a systematic cloze is to omit every *n*th (fifth, or seventh, or tenth, etc.) word throughout the text; usually every eighth or ninth word works well. A systematic cloze could also be prepared where certain word types are omitted. For example, all articles or all pronouns could be omitted. If the eye movements of a reader have been recorded, you could create a third type of systematic cloze by omitting the words the reader did not fixate.

**Procedure:** Begin by discussing Juan Antonio's reading and fixations. After this discussion, pass out the cloze procedure you have prepared. Students can work to read through the passages and fill in missing words individually or in groups. After students have finished, it is important to discuss their choices and the strategies they used to make those decisions. Cambourne and Y. Goodman (1996) have developed Cooperative Cloze, in which groups of two or three readers work together to fill in the blanks left in a story. The important thing is for students to really discuss their word choice and the difficulty of filling in the different slots. When students finish filling in the words of the story, they should always go back to see if there are any words they want to change. Students will often find that information from later parts of the story will help them come up with better answers for blanks in earlier sections. Students should also be encouraged to talk about specific cues that helped them make their decisions. Students will have an opportunity to learn from each other during these discussions. Less proficient readers will get insights into how more proficient readers make sense of text. You may want to pass out the completed original passage once students have finished so that students can compare their stories with what the author wrote. Often, students will find that they like their stories best. This can help students see that reading is a process of making our own meaning, not somebody else's.

## Selection of Predictable Text

Cloze procedures are helpful as exercises and illustrations of the reading process, but it's important to involve students in reading authentic (unaltered) text as much as possible. That doesn't mean that all texts are alike, however. Some texts lend themselves to developing readers' use of context and prediction more than others. To help teachers guide readers toward selecting texts that support the process of prediction, Freeman and Freeman (2000, 40) have created a checklist that details specific characteristics of texts that support reading.

### Characteristics of Text That Support Reading

1. Are the materials authentic? Authentic materials are written to inform or entertain, not to teach a grammar point or a letter-sound correspondence.
2. Are the materials predictable? Prediction is based on the use of repetitive patterns, cumulative patterns, rhyme, alliteration, and rhythm. Books are also predictable if students have background knowledge about the concepts presented.
3. Is there a good text-picture match? A good match provides nonlinguistic visual cues. Is the placement of the pictures predictable?
4. Are the materials interesting, imaginative, or both? Interesting, imaginative texts engage students.
5. Do the situations and characters in the book represent the experiences and backgrounds of the students in the class? Culturally relevant texts engage students.

## Cultural Relevance Rubric

A century of eye movement research has shown that the more unfamiliar a text is, the more readers' eye movements show signs of confusion and tentativeness. The corollary to those findings is that the more familiar a text is to a reader, the more efficient his or her eye movements become. Familiarity doesn't necessarily mean a knowledge of a specific text, but it can be knowledge of the content and under-standing of the background of the text's characters, setting, era, and so on. So one way teachers can help students improve their reading skills is by helping them select texts that are appropriate for their age, inter-ests, and cultural background and then encouraging readers to think about how their own lives relate to the characters' lives. Reading texts that are familiar to the reader helps build confidence and awareness of text structures.

One important characteristic of predictable texts that Freeman and Freeman list is cultural relevance, and a tool that is helpful for selec-tion of texts that connect with the readers' background is the Cultural Relevance Rubric (Freeman, Freeman, and Freeman 2003; see Figure 2–12). This rubric helps us see that there is much more to cultural rel-evance than the ethnicity of the characters in a text. There are multi-ple aspects of a text and of a reader's background to consider when looking for a good match. Cultural relevance of text is especially important to consider when choosing texts that will be used for assess-ment purposes. A text is more predictable for a reader when a teacher or student is able to mark mostly fours on this rubric.

**Preparation:**   Make an overhead of the rubric and a copy for each student. (A full-size reproducible can be found at www.heinemann. com/paulsonfreeman.)

**Procedure:**   Show your students an overhead of the Cultural Relevance Rubric. Discuss the idea of predictability of text and encourage students to think about why texts that we can relate to are easier to read. Carefully talk through each of the eight indicators for cultural relevance that are listed on the rubric.

You can then use this rubric to help students select predictable texts for general reading or for assessment purposes. For general reading, you can sit with students and skim through books. Together you can get a general idea of the cultural relevance of the texts and then select the most appropriate books to read. If the text is then used for assess-ment, students should fill in the rubric after reading. Student scores on the rubric should be taken into account along with their reading. You should expect a more proficient reading when a student scores mostly fours on the rubric.

## Cultural Relevance Rubric

1. Are the characters in the story like you and your family?

   Just like us . . . . . . . . . . . . . . . . . . . . . . . Not at all like us

   | 4 | 3 | 2 | 1 |

2. Have you lived in or visited places like those in the story?

   Yes . . . . . . . . . . . . . . . . . . . . . . . . . . . . . . . . No

   | 4 | 3 | 2 | 1 |

3. Could this story take place this year?

   Yes . . . . . . . . . . . . . . . . . . . . . . . . . . . . . . . . No

   | 4 | 3 | 2 | 1 |

4. How close do you think the main characters are to you in age?

   Very close . . . . . . . . . . . . . . . . . . . . . . . Not close at all

   | 4 | 3 | 2 | 1 |

5. Does the story have main characters who are boys (for boy readers)? Girls (for girl readers)?

   Yes . . . . . . . . . . . . . . . . . . . . . . . . . . . . . . . . No

   | 4 | 3 | 2 | 1 |

6. Do the characters talk like you and your family do?

   Yes . . . . . . . . . . . . . . . . . . . . . . . . . . . . . . . . No

   | 4 | 3 | 2 | 1 |

7. How often do you read stories like this one?

   Often . . . . . . . . . . . . . . . . . . . . . . . . . . . . . Never

   | 4 | 3 | 2 | 1 |

8. Have you ever had an experience like one described in this story?

   Yes . . . . . . . . . . . . . . . . . . . . . . . . . . . . . . . . No

   | 4 | 3 | 2 | 1 |

Figure 2–12

## *Readers Making Links to the Text*

As we have demonstrated with the Cultural Relevance Rubric, readers are more successful when they can connect with text. It is much easier to make predictions about what is coming up in a text when we can relate to it. This strategy helps readers think carefully about the characters and setting of a story and make personal connections with them. These connections are important, as they help readers attend to the context in the story and make informed predictions.

**Preparation:** Make copies of the following Links Guide for each student. Also make an overhead of the Links Guide and of the Cultural Relevance Rubric. Next, choose a well-known story that you, as the teacher, can make some connections with. Think about how your life connects to one of the characters and settings described in the story. A book that we've had fun using is Judith Viorst's *Alexander and the Terrible, Horrible, No Good, Very Bad Day* (1972). This is a story about a young boy who goes through a day when absolutely everything seems to go wrong.

**Procedure:** Begin by talking with your students about the importance of making connections with the text they are reading. You may wish to use a copy of the Cultural Relevance Rubric to help guide your discussion. Next, bring up a well-known story. Alternatively, do a shared reading or a read-aloud of a familiar story. Choose a character from the story and explain to the students how that character links to your life. When using *Alexander and the Terrible, Horrible, No Good, Very Bad Day* with classes, Ann compares herself with Alexander and talks with her students about unfortunate things that have happened to her. A typical modeling of this follows:

> "See how Alexander gets stuck squished in the middle seat of the car? Every morning I squeeze into a taxi with four other teachers to get to school. Sometimes it's really hard when I have lots of bags with me. I can imagine how annoyed Alexander must have been during his car ride!"

> "Poor Alexander ends up with a dessertless lunch! I almost never have a dessert in my lunch. In fact, I usually leave my apartment in such a rush that I forget my lunch altogether! I can understand how hungry and frustrated Alexander must have been."

## Links Guide

*Character Link*

*Make a link between one of the characters and your life. What is the link?*

| Character you made a link with: | The link: |
| --- | --- |
| | |

*After making this link, try seeing the story through that character's eyes.*

*Setting Link*

*Make a link between the setting and some place you can relate to in your life.*

| Setting you made a link with: | The link: |
| --- | --- |
| | |

Once you have modeled these types of connections for your class, ask a few students to do the same with either the same character or another from the story you have selected. Write their responses on the Links Guide overhead. (A full-size reproducible can be found at www.heinemann.com/paulsonfreeman.) Explain that once they can make this connection, it is interesting to think about the story from that character's point of view.

Follow the same format for discussing the setting of the story. Model this by making a connection with the setting and your life as Ann did for the character link. As with the character link, have a few students make connections with the setting of the story you are using orally and record their responses on the overhead. Once students have made these links with your guidance and have shared them as a group, they are ready to try this activity on their own. You can have copies of the Links Guide available for students to fill in as they read independently or as they work in literature study groups.

# Chapter 3

## Getting Inside the Reading Process: Do We Read Word-by-Word?

In Chapter 2 we discussed the number of words that are fixated (looked at) while reading. You could think of this as one piece of the puzzle of understanding the reading process. Readers don't look at every word when they read, thanks to the predictive nature of the reading process. But what about the fixations that *are* made—what order are they in? Think about your own reading. Is it all left-to-right, top-to-bottom, or are there some backward eye movements—called regressions—that take you to a previously viewed part of the sentence (or a part that was skipped) or a previous paragraph? The question, in reading theory terms, becomes Is reading a process of sequential word recognition?

Even with our knowledge that readers fixate only 50 percent to 75 percent of the words in a text, intuitively it still makes sense that whatever words we do look at, we look at in order. After all, we *understand* them in order, so it stands to reason that we look at them in order as well. Gough's view that "[the reader] plods through the sentence, letter by letter, word by word" (1972, 354) echoes this intuition, as does Adams and Bruck's understanding that "for skillful adult readers, meaningful text, regardless of its ease or difficulty, is read through what is essentially a left to right, line by line, word by word process" (1995, 11). Certainly, when we are reading, we have the perception that it is a left-to-right, line-by-line, word-by-word process. As we've seen, however, perceptions do not always have a one-to-one correspondence with the data from eye movement research.

Look back at Tim's example and the question in Chapter 1 about the direction of the eye movements. If you counted all the regressions—right-to-left eye movements—you found that about 17 percent of the fixations were regressions. The excerpt below (Figure 3–1) examines the regressions in the last part of the sentence

"Well, sitting here in the living room is a lot better than doing what I did the last time Bill was away overnight!"

I did the last time Bill was away overnight!
37    36 38 40    39 41    42    43 45    44    46

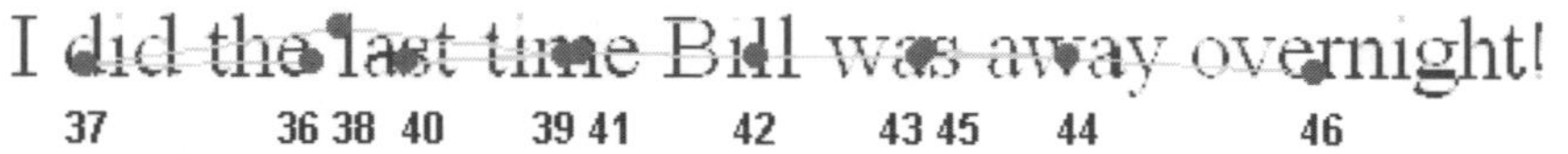

Figure 3–1

Tim first fixates on THE, then on DID, then on LAST, on to TIME, then back to LAST, and so on. We'll talk about oral reading miscues in the next chapter, but for our purposes here, it's important to understand that in this part of the sentence, Tim read it exactly as written. Thus, Tim *read aloud*:

"I did the last time Bill was away overnight!"

The words he *looked at*, however, were fixated in this order:

THE DID LAST TIME LAST TIME BILL WAS AWAY WAS OVERNIGHT.

In this order, the text is syntactic and semantic gibberish, yet Tim orally produced the sentence verbatim to the text.

Based on Tim's example, it doesn't seem necessary to look at each word in a strict left-to-right sequence in order to comprehend and produce a coherent text. Eye movement research supports this idea that regressions are an expected part of reading, comprising, on average, 10 percent to 20 percent of all fixations (Rayner and Pollatsek 1989, 432). This basic fact about reading should not be ignored, but it frequently is. Hogaboam (1983, 314–15) points out that

Models assuming this [sequential word-by-word] characterization of eye movements might be disregarding over three-fourths of the normal eye movement data. . . . The point to be taken from this is that it is inaccurate to characterize skilled reading as a process of moving one's eyes forward from one word to the next with occasional regressions.

One of the reasons regressions are interesting is because they are direct and instant indications of cognitive and comprehending processes at work. Saccades are under cognitive control (Rayner and Pollatsek 1989), so there is no delay between the desire to reexamine parts of the text and the ability to do so. Regressions are, therefore, instant responses to the text, probably usually for confirmation or disconfirmation purposes. As Underwood and Batt point out, "Regressive fixations usually are launched to areas of the text that have caused linguistic confusion, or contain particularly complicated words" (1996, 146). Taylor and Taylor concur, stating, "Ambiguous, unexpected, complex, or important information, be it semantic or syntactic, can cause regressions" (1983, 134).

Figure 3–2 below demonstrates how Mike regresses to refixate the word *barge*, a trouble area for him:

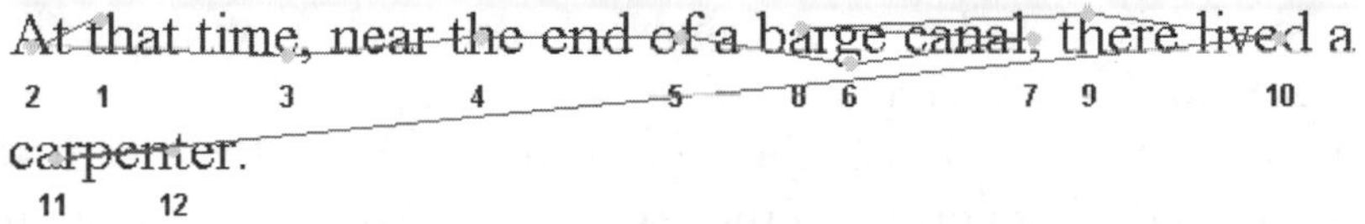

At that time, near the end of a barge canal, there lived a
 2   1        3          4         5    8 6      7  9        10
carpenter.
 11    12

Figure 3–2

*Barge* is a potential trouble area here for readers, as it is not a common word outside of port cities and is usually used as a noun, not a noun modifier. For these reasons, Mike might not have expected to find such a word in the text, and his eye movements show he is working to fit the concept into his schema. He fixates OF, then BARGE, then the punctuation between *canal* and *there* before regressing to BARGE and fixating it for more than twice his average word fixation duration. He then fixates THERE and makes only forward fixations for the remainder of the sentence.

In the following example (Figure 3–3), Judy regresses and refixates an entire phrase:

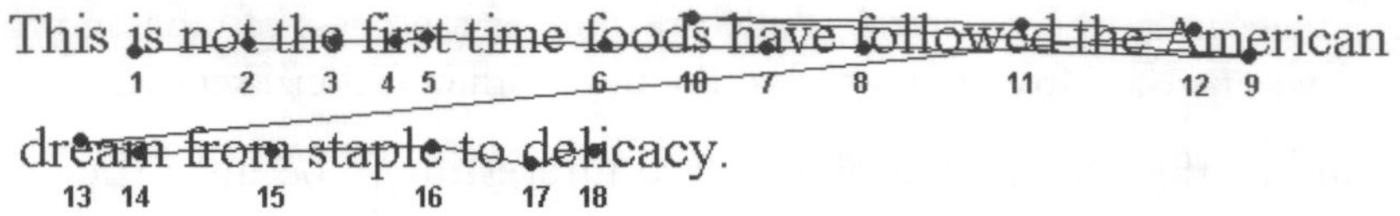

This is not the first time foods have followed the American
dream from staple to delicacy.

Figure 3–3

She executes two series of forward fixation sequences, joined by a single regression: she fixates IS, NOT, THE, FIRST, FOODS, HAVE, FOLLOWED, AMERICAN, then regresses to refixate FOODS, FOLLOWED, and AMERICAN. She fixates 75 percent of the words in this sentence, a high rate for her (her overall rate is 60.75 percent), which indicates tentativeness. She *refixates* three words in the same order that she first fixated them, giving the impression of a confirmation strategy or perhaps of changing the emphasis she gave portions of the sentence during the first pass.

Andrea, who is a proficient fourth-grade bilingual reader, tends to make regressions that help her along as she reads. The types of regressions Andrea makes suggest that she is confirming or double-checking what she has read. As Figure 3–4 shows, Andrea makes two regressions in this Spanish text excerpt.

In order to clearly display the regressions, we have shown only the fixations on the last portion of the text. The first regression, from fixation 3 to fixation 4, spans across almost two lines of print. This regression occurred as Andrea looked back to confirm something she had read previously, specifically, that the main character's teacher has written *Mary Lopez* on the inside cover of her book. In the text read by Andrea, *Mary Lopez* is italicized and appears almost as though the teacher had written it. As Andrea reads on, she comes to the words *La letra de la maestra (The teacher's handwriting)*. At that point in the text, Andrea regresses to fixate just below the italicized *Mary Lopez*. Here, Andrea's regression suggests that Andrea is comprehending the text as she looks back to confirm what was written in the teacher's handwriting.

Andrea's eye movements in this section of text capture a clear example of a reader interacting with the text during reading. Andrea did not passively scan across the page, putting words together to make sentences. Andrea fixated particular sections of text to create

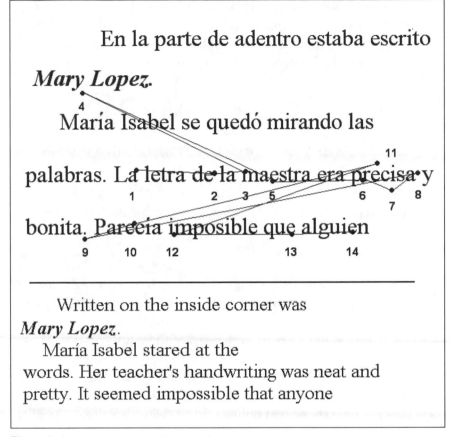

En la parte de adentro estaba escrito

*Mary Lopez.*

4
María Isabel se quedó mirando las

11
palabras. La letra de la maestra era precisa y

1          2    3    5              6      8
7

bonita. Parecía imposible que alguien

9      10      12              13      14

Written on the inside corner was
*Mary Lopez*.
María Isabel stared at the
words. Her teacher's handwriting was neat and
pretty. It seemed impossible that anyone

Figure 3–4

her own understanding of the author's message. She picked up on the author's use of italics to represent the handwriting of the teacher and was curious to look back at it. Through her eye movements, we can begin to get a sense of what Andrea might have been thinking as she interacted with this text.

Andrea's second regression shown in Figure 3–4 is a regression from fixation 10 to fixation 11. Here Andrea fixated the word PARECIA (SEEMED) and then regresses to fixate the word PRECIA (NEAT) on the previous line. These two words are graphically very similar, and it is possible that Andrea regressed in order to confirm that these were indeed two different words.

Regressions, however, can also indicate places where readers are having difficulty and perhaps are relying too much on the visual information from the text. Figure 3–5 below shows a sentence from an English text in which Jazmin made three regressive fixations.

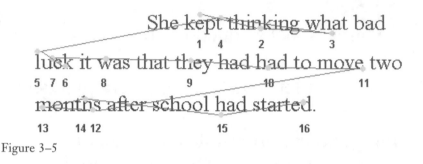

Figure 3–5

In this sentence, Jazmin's first regression involves the word KEPT and is from fixation 3 (under the word WHAT) to fixation 4 (in the space between KEPT and THINKING). Her second regression is on the word LUCK, where Jazmin moves from the end of the word (fixation 6) back to the middle of the word (fixation 7). Her last regression on this sentence is on the word MONTHS, where Jazmin fixates the end of the word (fixation 12) and then regresses to the beginning of it (fixation 13). This example shows that unlike Andrea, who regressed to confirm her predictions during comprehending, Jazmin is less efficient in her use of regressions. Her intraword regressions appear to be an attempt to overanalyze the graphic cues of the words.

So regressions happen, as a normal part of the reading process. But we shouldn't limit ourselves to thinking that regressions only go back a couple of words on a line. The excerpt in Figure 3–6 shows a regression Victoria, an adult reader, made across a column of text when reading a book review (Freeman 2001). Note that this is only an excerpt of her total fixations; the fixations in the first column are not superimposed onto the text, so that you can see where she made the regression.

As Victoria read through the first column for the first time (as mentioned earlier, those eye movements are not shown for purposes of clarity), she miscued on the word *touted* and then exclaimed "Oy!" possibly because she was not familiar with that word. Victoria then went

sion, and critical thinking. Separate chapters on writing, cooperative learning and multiculturalism (cultural and linguistic diversity) follow, appropriately placed in the final third of the book. Further, each of these sections not only provides the same variety of instructional practices with which earlier chapter are replete, but also reflects and advocacy position. The chapter on writing, for example, urges teachers to incorporate writing as much and as often as possible, recognizes the evaluation burden such writing places on the teacher, and provides several ways this can be minimized. Approaches to cooperative learning are touted as noncompetitive models of interaction, which teach skills student will need throughout their lives.

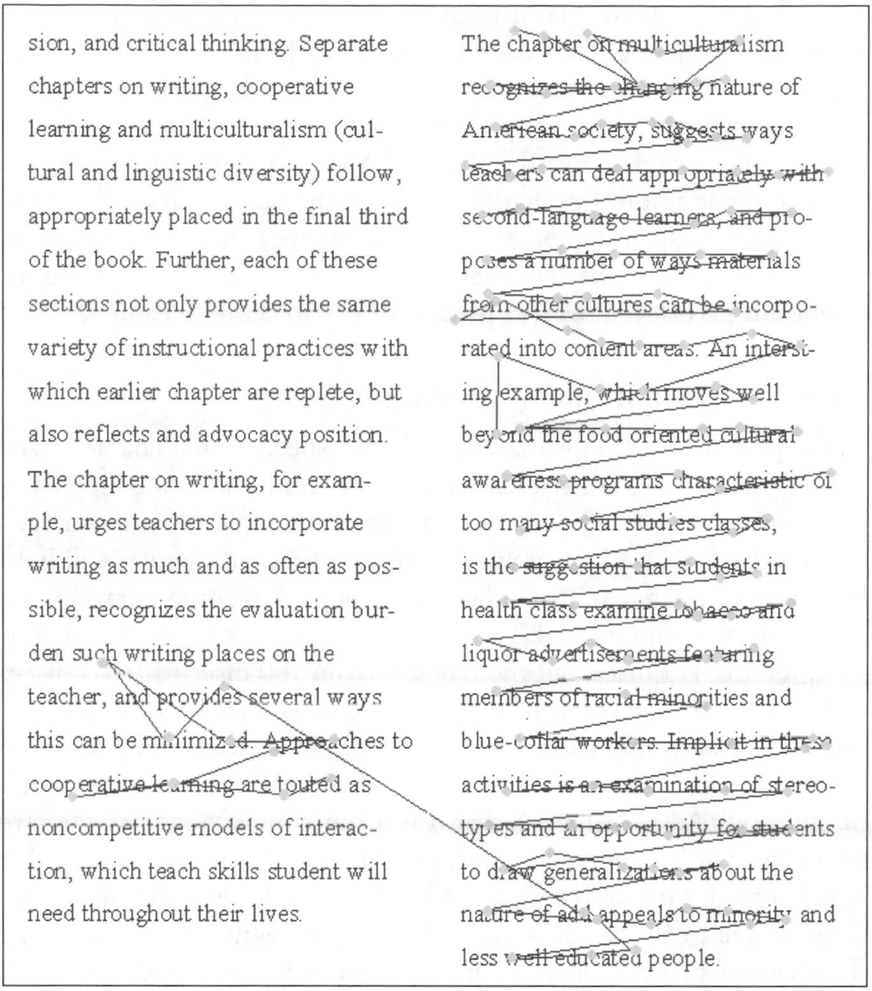

The chapter on multiculturalism recognizes the changing nature of American society, suggests ways teachers can deal appropriately with second-language learners, and proposes a number of ways materials from other cultures can be incorporated into content areas. An interesting example, which moves well beyond the food oriented cultural awareness programs characteristic of too many social studies classes, is the suggestion that students in health class examine tobacco and liquor advertisements featuring members of racial minorities and blue-collar workers. Implicit in these activities is an examination of stereotypes and an opportunity for students to draw generalizations about the nature of ad appeals to minority and less well educated people.

Figure 3–6

on to read the second column. Before she turned to the next page, however, there was a slight pause in her oral reading. Her eye movements show that during this oral pause, she regressed to reread the section of text in the previous column leading up to the word *touted*. Here again we see a reader interacting with text. After reading the word *touted*, Victoria perhaps decided that she would figure out what it meant by reading on. Once she got to the end of the second paragraph, she either understood the word and wanted to take a look at it again or was still unclear as to what it meant and wanted to reread the section up to the word to gather more information. Either way, we see that Victoria was actively interacting with this text as she made meaning.

Eye movement data clearly show that the process of reading is not limited to a straightforward letter-by-letter, word-by-word sequence of word recognition. But neither is it as simple as a couple of regressions at evenly spaced intervals. Regressions are made in order to disambiguate parts of the text that a reader struggles with and are an important part of the reader's process of constructing meaning.

## How Long Are Readers' Fixations?

In the previous section we saw that the perspective that characterizes reading as a process of sequential word recognition is not supported by readers' use of regressions as an important part of the reading process. Let's take a look at another piece of the puzzle that will help inform our understandings of how readers read: fixation duration.

The average duration of Tim's fixations in the excerpt presented in Chapter 1 is 413 msec, but the range is from 100 msec to 1,283 msec, with a standard deviation of 227 msec. This is a fairly wide range of durations and further supports the idea that the eyes don't merely skip across the text at a regular, predetermined rate. What causes this range in duration? Adams suggests that it is a function of how many letters are in the word: "The strongest determinant of the amount of time for which a reader fixates on a word is its length in letters, and this seems directly due to the visual labor required to recognize it" (1990, 101). This view explains differences in duration in terms of the amount of time it takes to see each letter in the word, with longer words necessarily taking more time. Thus, Tim would spend a longer time fixating the word *better* on the third line than the word IS on the same line, because *better* is three times as long as IS. However, Tim looks at BETTER for 267 msec and *is* for 683 msec—exactly the opposite of what should have happened. There are enough other examples (four-letter READ on line 7 for 800 msec, eight-letter BATHROOM on line 5 for 383 msec, etc.) to suggest the answer for duration differences lies elsewhere. If reading were simply a matter of fixating on a word long enough to process its component letters before moving on to the next word, words with the same amount of letters would be fixated for the same amount of time. Obviously, this is not the case. What, then, accounts for the difference in fixation durations between words?

In Chapter 2, we saw that prediction explains why some words aren't fixated, and this same concept has been proposed as a reason for the varying lengths of time different words are fixated. To test the effects of the predictability of text, Rayner and Well (1996) asked readers to read sentences that contained a target word that was either classified as high-, medium-, or low-constraint (i.e., very predictable, somewhat predictable, or less predictable). For this experiment, in order to determine the predictability of several target words in their texts, judges who did not participate in the study were given a cloze task with the sentence or paragraph presented up to the target word and asked to fill in the blank. Target words that were produced by the judges more than 60 percent of the time were considered highly constrained, or predictable, and target words that were produced less than 10 percent of the time were considered unconstrained. Eighteen readers' eye movements were recorded reading a range of sentences, from highly constrained to relatively unconstrained, with word length and word frequency controlled. The study's results indicate that the low-constraint words yielded longer fixation times than the medium- and high-constraint words, and readers were more likely to not fixate on the high-constraint target word than the medium- or low-constraint target word. The researchers conclude that "as far as fixation times of words are concerned, words that are unconstrained by context are fixated longer than words that are moderately to highly constrained" (507). In other words, the more a reader expected a given word, the shorter her fixation duration on that word would be.

Other eye movement researchers concur with Rayner and Well's findings; for example, in 1998, Reichle et al. stated that

> reading is a more interactive process, and there may be many situations in which a word will not be predictable in the absence of any information but quite predictable given minimal information such as approximate word length and the first letter. (53)

Factors that influence fixation duration include the level of predictability of the text and whether or not the reader's expectations were confirmed by the upcoming information. In short, readers constantly make predictions about upcoming text. Eye movement studies show that when readers encounter words that they expect, they need not fixate or they fixate for a shorter time than when faced with an unexpected word. Thus, a view of reading as a process of looking at each word, in order, with the length of that look dependent on the amount of letters in the word, is not supported by the information eye movement research provides about the duration of readers' fixations.

*Context and predictability*

## Summary

In this chapter we focused on the question of whether reading can be considered sequential word recognition. We looked at readers' regressions and how they are an important aspect of reading. After examining the duration of Tim's fixations, it is clear that readers do not simply skip across the text at a predetermined rate, but instead they look at different parts of the text for different periods of time. Evidence from our studies and other eye movement research furthers the idea that context and prediction play an important role in the reading process. In the following chapter, we add miscue analysis to the mix and examine what the visual data provided by eye movement recording and the verbal data provided by oral reading can combine to teach us about the reading process.

### Extension Questions

1. How is reading like or unlike a process of sequential word recognition; does it seem accurate to say that readers simply add up letters to comprehend words, add up words to comprehend sentences, and add up sentences to comprehend a text? What is an alternative to this view?

2. In Chapter 2, we saw how the eyes deliver what amounts to garbled graphic input to the brain. In this chapter, we saw that even when that happens, readers still produce oral readings that can be verbatim to the printed text. How does this inform your answer to question 1?

3. We've seen examples of regressions that include looking back to a previous part of the same word (an intraword regression), a previous part of the sentence, and a previous column of text. How is

each of these types of regressions different—what is the reader's purpose for making each type of regression?

4. We've seen that it's not necessarily the length of the word that determines how long a reader looks at that word. What would seem to be some of the factors that determine the duration of time spent on a given word?

5. As we have seen in this chapter, readers make regressions to various sections of text as they are comprehending text. During these regressions, there is often a pause in their oral reading. As a teacher, how might this knowledge change what you say or do when you hear a reader pause?

## Eye Movement Links to Reading Instruction

As we've discussed in this chapter, readers make regressions for a variety of comprehension-based reasons. They regress to clarify a word or phrase, to confirm or disconfirm a prediction, to make connections between different parts of the text, and so on. Haber and Hershenson point out that "the presence of such a large number of regressive movements, even in college students, poses a severe problem for any model that describes reading as progressing smoothly from left to right, picking up information from the text in the order in which it is presented" (1973, 220). We've seen what kind of visual information this presents to the reader, yet he is still able to construct meaning with the text; in fact, moving backward and moving forward—sampling the text—both appear to be necessary parts of the meaning construction process. The following strategies are predicated on our understanding of reading as more than a simple letter-by-letter, word-by-word process of recognition.

### Reading On: Khaen

Regressions are such an important part of the reading process that they shouldn't be ignored. However, there is another strategy often not utilized by readers that can be just as effective: reading on. While discussing regressions with readers, it's helpful to point out that if they are stuck on a word, going backward can help, but so can going in the other direction; that is, they can go *past* the word to try to figure it out as well. In other words, while meaning can be clarified by regressing, it can also be aided by reading on and gathering more information in order to make sense of the text. Goodman, Watson, and Burke (1996) provide a variety of strategy lessons that help readers discover meaning when reading; one of these in particular, a strategy using the word *petoskey*, a kind of fossil found on the shores of Lake Michigan, is an excellent tool for helping engender in students the confidence to read on to understand text. Below, we provide a similar strategy lesson using the word *khaen*, a wind instrument from Laos.

**Preparation:** Make an overhead transparency of the Khaen story. (A full-size reproducible can be found at www.heinemann.com/paulsonfreeman.) Have a blank overhead and marker or a board and marker ready to record class predictions.

## KHAEN

1. Peter bought Alex a khaen.
2. It was a gift for his birthday.
3. Peter brought it all the way back from Laos.
4. Khaen are very popular in Laos, northeast Thailand, northern Vietnam, and southern China.
5. There are several different types of khaen.
6. All of Alex's friends will get to enjoy the khaen.
7. Alex's new khaen is about three feet in length, which is smaller than some—they can be as big as six feet long!
8. Alex plans to use it for his storytelling performances.
9. Traditionally, khaen are used at social functions and religious ceremonies.
10. Alex's khaen is made out of a special bamboo.
11. Peter thinks Alex will have fun learning how to play his new khaen.
12. Khaen was given its name long ago by the governor of Laos. *Khaen* means "better," which refers to the instrument sounding better than any other the governor had ever heard.

13. Alex's khaen looks similar to a pan flute, with rows of long tubes bound together. There is a chamber made of wood that goes through the center of the tubes.
14. Alex holds the khaen with the pipes in a vertical position and blows through the mouthpiece to produce a sound that is like a cross between an accordion and a harmonica.
15. Western spellings include *khaen*, *khene*, and *kaen*, but the word is pronounced approximately "can," as in "tin can."

**Procedure:**    Place the Khaen overhead on the projector. Cover all of the statements except for the word *KHAEN* with a piece of paper. Show the students the word and ask them to predict what it could mean. Students will have different pronunciations of the word, which will make for interesting discussion. Because *khaen* is a real word, you may wish to begin by asking students not to tell the class if they do know what the word is. Have students brainstorm what the word might mean and list the predictions students make on the blank overhead or on the board. Next, have the class read the first statement under the title. Then have the students confirm or disconfirm their original predictions by adding or crossing off guesses from the class list. Continue to read each statement and edit the list as a class each time. Remember, it's not necessary to write *all* of the student's predictions after seeing the word for the first time; write only a few since you will be adding more as you go along. Keep it moving! For younger readers you may want to shorten the activity by selectively removing some of the sentence clues. The class will be able to use the clues to eventually understand what a khaen is.

It is important to provide time for students to discuss with classmates why they made certain predictions and what clues helped them confirm their predictions or helped them decide they had not made a good guess. Readers who are less proficient see that even the good readers don't know all the words. They also come to understand the process good readers use to make guesses about words they don't know. All of the students will discover that sounding out words like *khaen* won't help them make sense of it at all. Finally, they will start to see that reading on for more information is an effective strategy for making meaning. As an extension, it is fun to have students come up with uncommon words and make up their own "read on" strategy activity to share with the class.

A second extension to this strategy can be done with students who are engaged in literature circles. Have students place sticky notes on unknown words they come across as they are reading independently. As they read on, ask them to place sticky notes on 8words or phrases that helped them understand what the unknown words were. Students can share what they learned with classmates during their literature circle discussion time.

Analyses of readers' eye movements show several strategies readers use to make sense of the text. They regress and reread words or phrases (or more), connect parts of the text to other parts, as we saw Andrea do earlier in this chapter, skip words, fixate some words several times, and so on. These are microstrategies readers use naturally—they move their eyes around the text, forward and backward, skipping sections, rereading sections, looking at whatever part of the text helps them gather information about the text. One charge that teachers have is to take readers' natural strategies—these flicks of the eye—and formalize them as strategies the readers are cognitively aware of and thus can make greater use of. The following three ideas can be used to discuss reading strategies with students. The Strategy Ruler can be used with younger students and the Scanning Protocol and the Great 8 can be used with adolescent and older readers.

## The Strategy Ruler

The Strategy Ruler was developed by Gopa Goswami when she was working in an elementary school with young readers. Gopa wanted to help students think about the strategies they use as readers and have immediate access to them as they read. While many classrooms have lists of strategies posted around the room, when each student has his own Strategy Ruler, teachers can help individuals focus on the strategies that are most useful to them.

**Preparation:**   Cut pieces of 8.5-by-11 inch construction paper into thirds lengthwise. Have one length of construction paper and four small sticky notes available for each student. Make an overhead of the figure showing Angel's eye movements (Figure 3–7). (A full-size reproducible can be found at www.heinemann.com/paulsonfreeman.)

**Procedure:**   Begin with a discussion of how our eyes move around text in order to make sense of it. Show students the overhead of Angel's eye movements and describe what his eyes are doing as he reads.

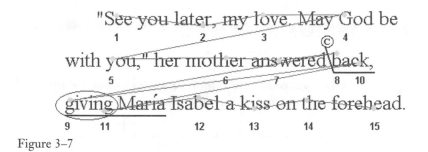

Figure 3–7

This is what Angel read aloud:

"'See you later, my love. May God be with you,' her mother answered back, María, back giving María Isabel a kiss on the forehead."

Encourage students to think about how Angel was able to read this section of text without looking at every word. Describe Angel's miscue: he omitted the word *giving* after having looked right at it. Instead of reading the word aloud the first time he saw it, he skipped it and read the next word, *María*. When that didn't make sense to him, he went back to the word *back*, read it again to get a running start and then read the word *giving* and the rest of the section with no problem. Angel used two good strategies here: (1) skipping and reading on and (2) rereading to get a running start.

Ask students to think about the strategies they use when they come to hard parts or words they don't know when they are reading. Generate a class list of strategies on a large piece of paper. It might be helpful to show additional eye movement examples to help students come up with strategies like "just skip it" or "go back and reread the section." Once the class has come up with several strategies, ask students to think about four strategies that they would like to try during their silent reading time. Have students write each of their four strategies on a separate sticky note and place the notes across their piece of construction paper. Explain to your students that they should have their Strategy Rulers with them when they are reading. If they get stuck, they should look at their ruler and try the first strategy. They should continue to try the strategies until they come to one that works to help them with that section of text.

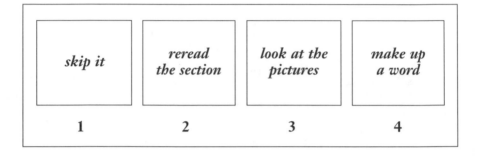

You may notice that some students overrely on certain strategies. Many students, for example, will always try to sound it out first. Help these students arrange their strategies so that "sound it out" is the last strategy on their ruler. Placing strategies such as "skip it" or "look at the pictures" first would be helpful.

## Scanning Protocol

As we have suggested with the cloze procedure and the Strategy Ruler, it is helpful to show your class an example of a student's actual eye movements in order to discuss the reading process. Eric uses this Scanning Protocol to show his students what proficient readers do to preview new material. As we discussed in this chapter, readers do not look at each word on the page in order or for the same length of time. This is often surprising to older students who try to plod word-by-word through their difficult textbooks. This strategy targets secondary readers and is useful for any teacher concerned with content literacy.

**Preparation:** Make an overhead projector transparency of the example in Figure 3–8 and copies of the "blank" (no eye movements) textbook

of the whole body, it is evident that what should be first developed is a general physical efficiency.

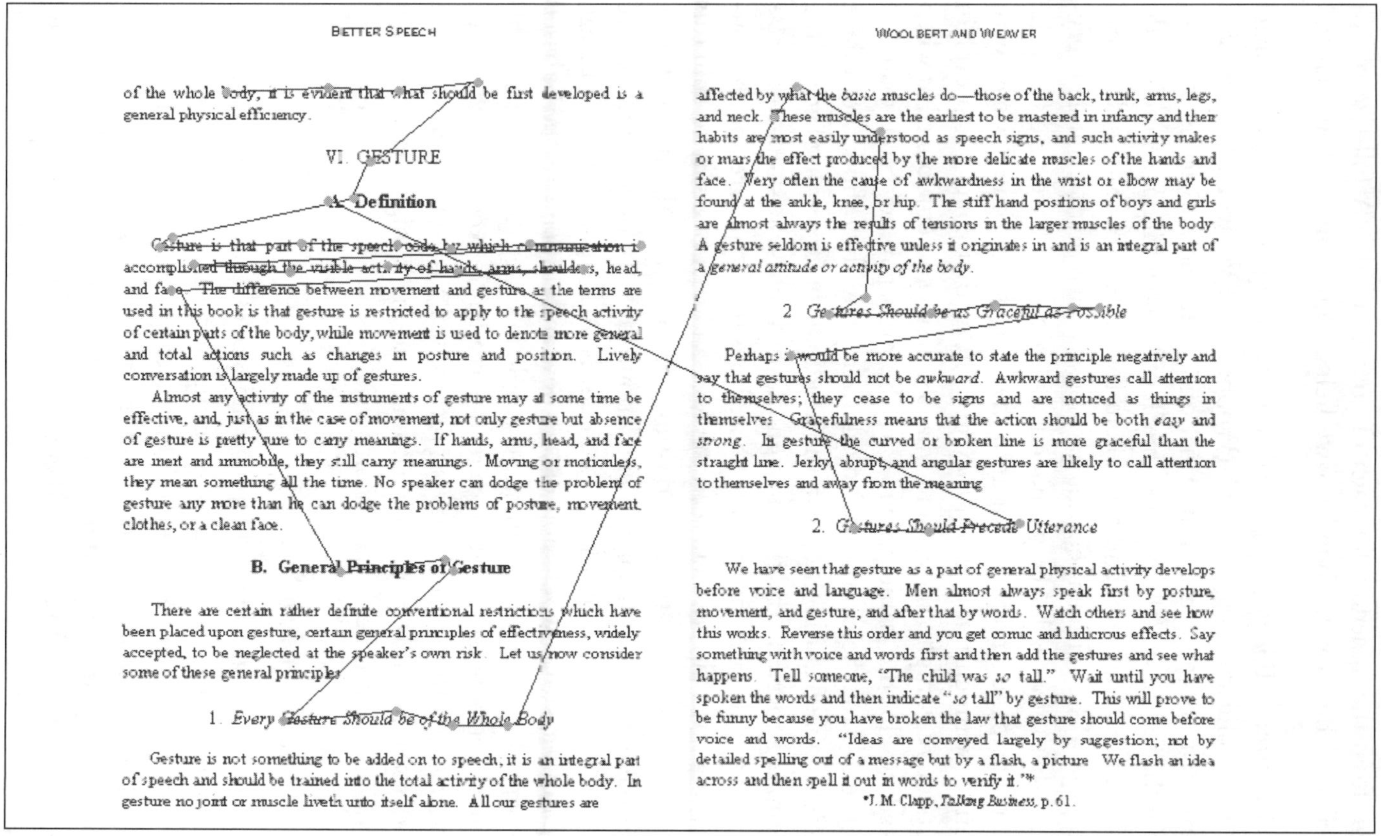

## VI. GESTURE

### A. Definition

Gesture is that part of the speech code by which communication is accomplished through the visible activity of health, arms, shoulders, head, and face. The difference between movement and gesture as the terms are used in this book is that the gesture is restricted to apply to the speech activity of certain parts of the body, while movement is used to denote more general and total actions such as changes in posture and position. Lively conversation is largely made up of gestures.

Almost any activity of the instruments of gesture may at some time be effective, and, just as in the case of movement, not only gesture but absence of gesture is pretty sure to carry meanings. If hands, arms, head, and face are inert and immobile, they still carry meanings. Moving or motionless, they mean something all the time. No speaker can dodge the problem of gesture any more than he can dodge the problems of posture, movement clothes, or a clean face.

### B. General Principles of Gesture

There are certain rather definite conventional restrictions which have been placed upon gesture, certain general principles of effectiveness, widely accepted, to be neglected at the speaker's own risk. Let us now consider some of these general principle.

#### 1. *Every Gesture Should Be of the Whole Body*

Gesture is not something to be added on to speech; it is an integral part of speech and should be trained into the total activity of the whole body. In gesture no joint or muscle liveth unto itself alone. All our gestures are affected by what the basic muscles do—those of the back, trunk, arms, legs, and neck. These muscles are the earliest to be mastered in infancy and their habits are most easily understood as speech signs, and such activity makes or mars the effect produced by the more delicate muscles of the hands and face. Very often the cause of awkwardness in the wrist or elbow may be found at the ankle, knee, or hip. The stiff hand positions of boys and girls are almost always the results of tensions in the larger muscles of the body. A gesture seldom is effective unless it originates in and is an integral part of *a general attitude or activity of the body.*

#### 2. *Gestures Should Be as Graceful as Possible*

Perhaps it would be more accurate to state the principle negatively and say that gestures should not be *awkward.* Awkward gestures call attention to themselves; they cease to be signs and are noticed as things in themselves. *Gracefulness* means that the action should be both *easy* and *strong.* In gesture the curved or broken line is more graceful than the straight line. Jerky, abrupt, and angular gestures are likely to call attention to themselves and away from the meaning.

#### 2. *Gestures Should Precede Utterance*

We have seen that gesture as a part of general physical activity develops before voice and language. Men almost always speak first by posture, movement, and gesture, and gesture, and after that by word. Watch others and see how this works. Reverse this order and you get comic and ludicrous effects. Say something with voice and words first and then add the gestures and see what happens. Tell someone, "The child was *so tall.*" Wait until you have spoken the words and then indicate "*so tall*" by gesture. This will prove to be funny because you have broken the law that gesture should come before voice and words. "Ideas are conveyed largely by suggestion, not by detailed spelling out of a message but by a flash, a picture. We flash an idea across and then spell it out in words to verify it."*

*J.M. Clapp, *Talking Business,* p. 61.

Figure 3-8

page from the appendix for each of your students. (A full-size reproducible of these can be found at www.heinemann.com/paulsonfreeman.)

**Procedure:**   Tell your students you are going to give them a page from a public speaking textbook (Woobert and Weaver 1922) and you want them to get as much information about that subject as they can from that page. But the catch is they'll only have fifteen seconds to do it. Hand the page out, and time them for fifteen seconds as they read the page. When fifteen seconds have passed, ask them to circle everything that they read. Many students will probably have read from the top of the page straight down until they ran out of time. Discuss with them how much information they got out of that page. Then explain that you're going to show them what a college student looked at when asked to do the same thing. Put the transparency you made of Figure 3–8 on the overhead and ask them why they think the college student looked at the title, then the headings, before going back to the beginning to read straight through. This discussion should progress toward the idea that previewing an author's text structure and the content of a text helps readers read the text, and that one way to gain this preview is through attention to titles, headings, and the first sentence in a section. Talk to your students about the idea of scanning text in order to get an idea of what the content is. Ask students to brainstorm a list of ways they would approach a new and difficult textbook based on what they've learned from the example in Figure 3–8. Have the students discuss where on the page the reader looked and where the reader spent the most time. Ask the students to reflect on why this reader scanned this way and what implications it might have for their own approach to new academic material.

## The Great 8 Reading Strategy

This guide is valuable in helping students effectively read and comprehend academic texts and is useful for secondary and postsecondary reading students and content area reading. The level is easily varied by the essay chosen to use in conjunction with the strategy. The step-by-step procedures help readers make predictions, make connections with the text, and ensure they are making sense of what they are reading.

# The Great 8 Guide

| Before Reading | | |
|---|---|---|
| identification | 1 | Write the title of the article here, and the subtitle, if there is one: |
| prediction | 2 | Just from the title, what do you think the *topic* of the article is? | Use 1 word OR 1 phrase: |
| background knowledge | 3 | Write three things you already know about the topic: | 1 <br> 2 <br> 3 |
| prediction | 4 | Just from the title, what do you think the article will be about (main idea)? | This article is *probably* about . . . |

| During Reading | | |
|---|---|---|
| attention | 5 | List 3 things you learn from the article, *while* reading it: | 1 <br> 2 <br> 3 |

| After Reading | | |
|---|---|---|
| comprehension | 6 | What is the article about (main idea)? | This article is about . . . |
| comparison | 7 | How is this similar or different from your answer for number 4, above? | |
| extension | 8 | List 3 questions you have about the article, or 3 things that could make the article better: | 1 <br> 2 <br> 3 |

Figure 3–9

**Preparation:** Make a copy of the Great 8 Guide (Figure 3–9) for each of your students. (A full-size reproducible can be found at www.heinemann.com/paulsonfreeman.) Also make one overhead of the guide. Select a short (one- to two-page) academic article or essay (*Time-* and *Newsweek*-type essays work well) and make copies for your students.

**Procedure:** Model the use of the Great 8 Guide by giving your class a copy of a short article and a copy of the Great 8 Guide. Using an overhead of the guide, work through items 1 through 4 as a class. Ask for volunteers to answer the questions and write the answers on the overhead. When you get to item 5, ask the students to read the article silently on their own. As they read, they should write down three things they have learned. Once the students are done reading, ask volunteers to share what they learned during the reading. Write three of the ideas on the overhead. Next, as a class, work through the final three items.

After filling in the Great 8 Guide, have your students talk about how it affected their reading and comprehension of the article. Ask which sections were easy and which were difficult to fill in. Have the class think about which sections of the article they spent more time on in order to fill in the guide and how this helped them make sense of the article. Once you have modeled the use of the Great 8 Guide with your class, encourage students to use this strategy sheet as they read articles on their own.

# *Chapter 4*

## *Making Sense of Text: Eye Movements and Miscue Analysis*

So far we've talked about several important aspects of reading that are demonstrated by the science of eye movement recording and analysis. Namely, that readers skip lots of words while they read and that where they do look—and how long they look there—is a function of the process of creating meaning from the text. It's a very fast process, so it's difficult to feel yourself doing it while you read, but nevertheless, eye movement research shows that the reader's eyes go to where the reader wants to gather information on a moment-by-moment basis.

At this point, you may be wondering about comprehension—how do we know that the readers we've been discussing are understanding the text they're looking at? After all, if they have no idea what they're reading, the eye movements could just be random. Eye movement researchers have struggled with this problem for years; Just and Carpenter (1984) pointed out that to have really effective eye movement data, it's useful to combine it with something else that lets you know what else the reader is doing in addition to moving her eyes.

For this reason, since at least the early 1920s (Buswell 1922), researchers have recorded readers reading aloud while their eye movements were recorded. It isn't until recently, however, that a method of analyzing the oral reading has been systematically applied to readers reading aloud in front of the eye tracker. In the last few years, there have been several dissertations and studies published that have combined eye movement analysis with miscue analysis, an approach that has been termed EMMA (Eye Movement Miscue Analysis) in those publications (e.g., Paulson 2000, 2002; Freeman 2001; Duckett 2001, 2002).

Miscues are unexpected responses to the text that readers produce when reading a text aloud—usually substitutions, omissions, repetitions, and insertions. Substitutions involve a reader replacing a word in the text with a different one and are signified in miscue analysis by writing the reader's word above the word it replaced, like this:

*substitution*
word.

Nonword substitutions—places where a reader replaces a text word with a word that doesn't exist—are signified by a $ sign directly in front of the nonword substitution. Omissions describe a reader's exclusion of a word from the text, verbally "skipping over" that word, and are denoted by placing a circle around the omitted word:

word.

As the name implies, repetitions refer to when readers repeat a word, phrase, or more and are indicated by the symbol ® with a line drawn under the words that were repeated:

®
this is an example of a repetition.

When readers verbally put in a word that is not in the written text, that is called an insertion. Insertions are signified by a caret placed where the word was inserted, pointing to the inserted word:

*insertion*
word ∧ word.

For a thorough introduction to miscues and miscue analysis, see Goodman, Watson, and Burke (1987) or Wilde (2000). In Figure 4–1, Jazmin provides an example of substitution-type miscues, including two nonword substitutions (indicated by the symbol $). Jazmin read aloud, "'You're see, you're like your new school,' her mother said. But her mother's safe, reasring vocie didn't seem to convince María Isabel."

What causes these miscues? Is it "carelessness," as Ekwall (1981) believes, or "failure of [the] pupil to scan the word thoroughly enough to identify the order of the letters and to be certain that the word is a particular word and not another" (Dechant 1981, 333)? A lack of enough visual input seems to be the commonly held understanding for

*You're      you're*
"You'll see, you'll like your new

                                      *mother*

school," her mother said. But her mother's

*safe   $reasring $vocie*
soft, reassuring voice didn't seem to

convince María Isabel.

Figure 4–1

why miscues are produced. In fact, entire studies have been constructed around the premise that substitutions occur when the reader doesn't see the word correctly. For example, Nicholson, Pearson, and Dykstra's 1979 study was designed to emulate certain miscues and assumed that when readers make oral substitutions, they have not seen the correct word, and they have failed to see at all the words that they omit:

> It was assumed that in trying to understand a story, the unskilled reader is not only faced with insufficient text data (caused by failing to respond at all to certain words) but anomalous data as well (caused by responding with certain semantically inappropriate substitutions). (341)

In addition, Smith (1994) explains away miscues in general as the by-products of a focus on meaning that allows the surface level of language a certain amount of carelessness:

> The prior use of meaning ensures that when individual words must be identified, for example, in order to read aloud, a minimum of visual information will be used. And as a consequence, mistakes will often occur. (154)

In general, the commonsense explanation for the generic causes of substitutions are carelessness, reading too rapidly, and not using enough visual information.

This commonsense explanation is logical—after all, we already know that we don't look at a certain amount of words while reading, as we saw in Chapter 2. So it stands to reason that the words that are miscued are also the ones that are skipped. Based on this, if we think back to Tim's example in Chapter 1, there are several candidates for miscues, since he skipped 28 percent of the words. Below (Figure 4–2) is an excerpt from that example, showing the first two lines. Tim orally omitted two words in the first two lines. Based on visual explanations, which two do you predict he omitted?

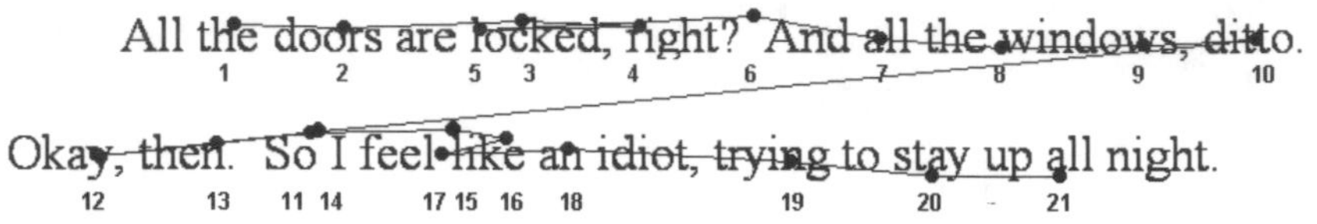

All the doors are locked, right? And all the windows, ditto.

Okay, then. So I feel like an idiot, trying to stay up all night.

Figure 4–2

Candidates would seem to include *all, are, and, the, idiot, up, night,* and others that were not fixated. However, Tim read all of those words verbatim! The two words he omitted were *all* (second sentence) and *then* (third sentence)—two words he looked right at! Now let's take a look at the miscues on the rest of his example (see Figure 4–3; a larger reproducible can be found at www.heinemann.com/paulsonfreeman).

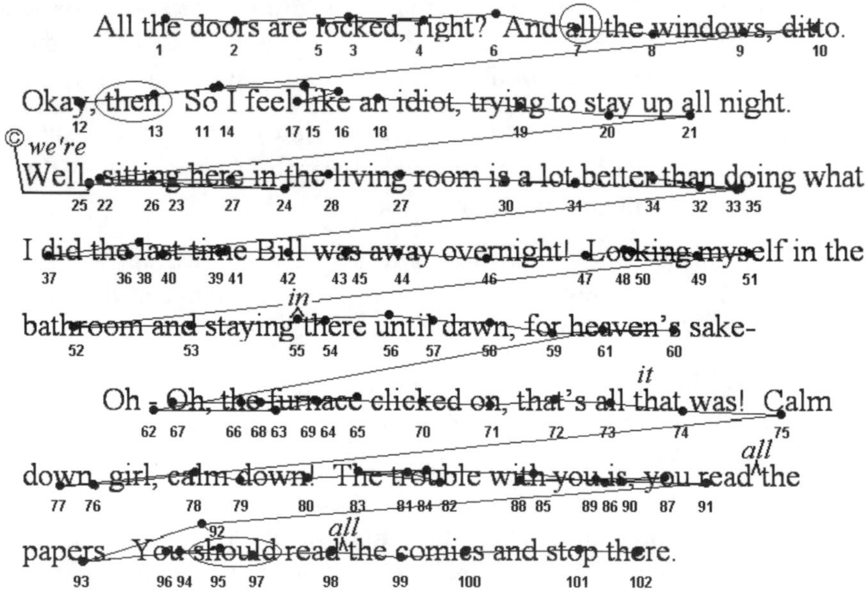

All the doors are locked, right? And all the windows, ditto.

Okay, then. So I feel like an idiot, trying to stay up all night.

*we're*
Well, sitting here in the living room is a lot better than doing what

I did the last time Bill was away overnight! Looking myself in the

*in*
bathroom and staying there until dawn, for heaven's sake-

*it*
Oh . Oh, the furnace clicked on, that's all that was! Calm

*all*
down, girl, calm down! The trouble with you is, you read the

*all*
papers. You should read the comics and stop there.

Figure 4–3

Tim made 8 miscues in this section, which comes out to about 8.5 miscues per hundred words—not at all unusual for a teenage reader. Three of his miscues were omissions, and they were all fixated. Tim made three insertions, twice inserting *all* after the word *read* and once inserting *in* between *staying* and *there*. Each time he inserted a word, he looked directly at at least one of the words adjacent to the insertion, and in the case of *in*, he looked right at the space between the words where he inserted *in*. Two of his miscues were substitutions: *we're* for *well* and *it* for *that*, and the word *that* was fixated, albeit right on the end of the word. The only miscue in this section that is not fixated is his substitution of *we're* for *well*—and, interestingly, that was the only miscue that he corrected! After making a return sweep from the previous line, Tim first fixated on the *s* of *sitting*, then on the *g* of *sitting*, then the *t* on *the*, then uttered "we're." Then, realizing something was not quite right, he looked back at the comma after *well*, corrects his miscue by saying *well*—then continued with the rest of the sentence. We could do a lot more analysis here that would provide a lot of information about Tim and his reading (for example, was the insertion of the second *all* part of Tim's efforts to maintain parallel construction in the text?). But let's consider readers other than Tim—is there a similar pattern of readers actually looking right at the words they miscue?

Let's look briefly at the eye movements for Jazmin's miscue example we introduced at the beginning of this chapter, where she makes six substitutions:

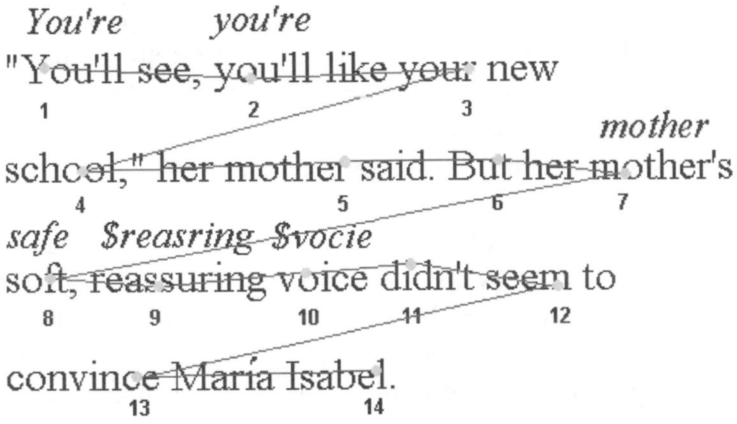

Figure 4–4

In Figure 4–4 above, Jazmin substitutes *you're* for the text item *you'll* each time it appears. On the second line she substitutes *mother* for *mother's*. On the third line, Jazmin makes three miscues. She substitutes *safe* for *soft* and then makes two nonword substitutions, *reasring* for *reassuring*, and *vocie* for *voice*. Although several words in that sentence were not fixated, all of these miscued words were fixated.

In Jazmin's example as well as Tim's excerpt, we see that the miscued words are not simply skipped, and eye movement research indicates that these examples are not flukes. For example, in one study, "readers were as likely to fixate a word they orally substituted or omitted as they were to fixate a word they produced verbatim to the text . . . the results of this study suggest that readers are likely to look directly at words they omit or substitute for an ample duration" (Paulson 2002, 62). Recent studies (Freeman 2001; Duckett 2001) and earlier research (Fairbanks 1937) have found similar results.

Freeman (2001), for example, found similar results when analyzing the miscues and eye movements of fourth-grade bilingual readers. "The data suggest that readers sample more visual information in both English and Spanish at places in the text where they miscue than at places where they don't miscue" (203). Freeman also found that "more time was spent on fixations on miscued words in both the Spanish and English texts than on non-miscued words" (218).

But what about very young students who are just beginning to learn to read? Duckett (2001), who studied beginning readers' use of pictures and print as they read age-appropriate picture books, found that even the first graders in his study spent time on miscued words. Duckett found that the readers in his study "fixated miscued words well beyond their personal average fixation duration prior to producing a miscue 94 percent of the time" (206).

So when your student makes an oral reading miscue, it is likely that he looked at that word and looked at it for a sufficient amount of time. Miscues are not caused by a lack of visual information. The answer to the question, What causes miscues? is beyond the scope of this book. For directions miscue research has taken, see Brown, Goodman, and Marek (1996). More useful for our purposes here is to move toward understanding what readers do while making a certain kind of miscue.

In the next section, we take an in-depth look at what goes on during a common oral reading miscue: repetitions.

## What Readers Do When They Make Repetitions

In the sentence in Figure 4–5 below, Sam, a teenage reader, repeated the word *for*:

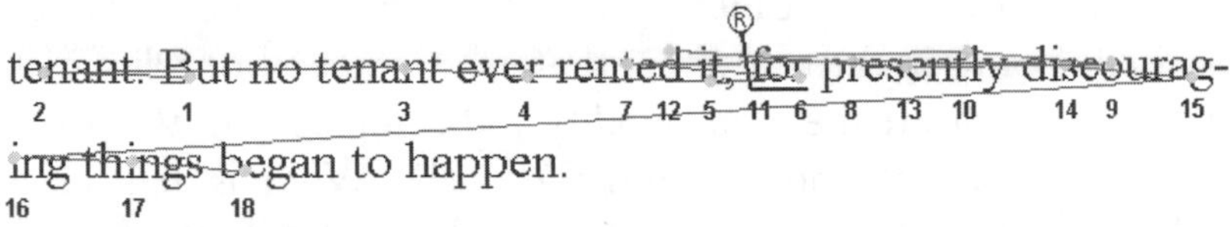

tenant. But no tenant ever rented it, for presently discouraging things began to happen.

Figure 4–5

Sam fixated FOR, then said "for" for the first time. He then regressed to RENTED, fixated forward to PRESENTLY, fixated forward to DISCOURAG-, regressed to refixate PRESENTLY, regressed again to refixate FOR, and regressed once more to RENTED. Sam then repeated "for." So between oral utterances of *for*, Sam produced a series of regressions and refixations. In this way, the repetition served as a place marker for Sam as he sampled the text heavily. After his repetition of *for*, Sam's eye movements were all forward-moving and he made no miscues during the remainder of the sentence. His relatively dense sampling of the text between repetitions of *for* seems to have been for confirmation and disconfirmation purposes. Apparently he was troubled by the use of *for* as a conjunction (meaning "because"), as he checked the expected syntax of the sentence; after the repetition, it was smooth sailing. In this example he fixated the repeated word and made an interesting regressive sequence between oral repetitions; that gives us insight into his process of assigning syntax to the sentence.

Words the reader orally repeats are fixated more often than other, nonmiscued words (Paulson 2000), an event that may in part be due to a high degree of tentativeness with that section of the text in general. This idea is supported by the unique miscue–eye movement relationship of repetitions (orally repeating a word) to regressions (looking back at a part of the text already viewed). That relationship is characterized by the fact that most repetitions involve a regressive sequence that takes place between oral utterances of the repeated word, an indication that repetitions are used for a specific purpose. Repetitions may be a type of cognitive strategy for dealing with a difficult or unexpected portion of text. In this sense, repetitions may be seen as an indication of comprehension processes at work.

Miscue research reveals that "the position, extent, and frequency of repetitions reflect the reader's lack of efficiency and confidence. Examining points in the text where the reader's repetitions diminish or increase may indicate the predictability and complexity of the passage" (Goodman, Watson, and Burke 1987, 151). What is less clear is whether the complexity lies in the word or phrase that is being repeated or in the text surrounding the repetition.

The answer may be both. Some repeated words and phrases receive direct regressions and multiple fixations, which indicates it is the repeated portion of the text that is causing problems for the reader. For example, in Figure 4–6 below, Mike fixates BARGE, and then says "barge," fixates the space between CANAL and THERE, refixates BARGE, and verbally repeats "barge," then finishes the sentence without any more regressions.

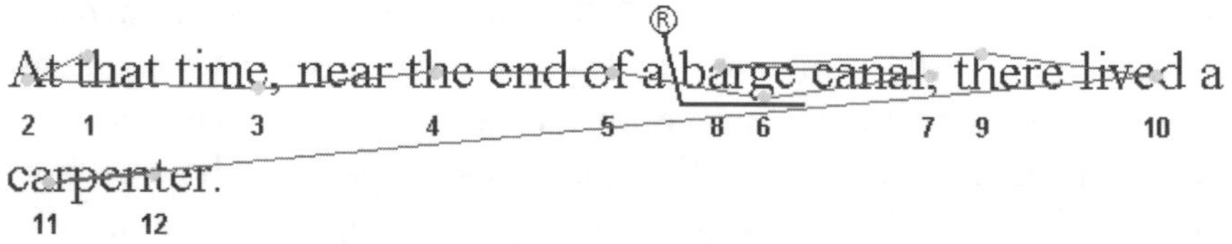

At that time, near the end of a barge canal, there lived a carpenter.

Figure 4–6

Clearly, Mike's repetition of the unusual type of canal is part of his strategy for processing the repeated word itself. He verbally produces "barge," fixates forward for a short period, then regresses and directly refixates BARGE. After he finishes his regressive sequence, he repeats "barge" and moves on. This type of repetition, where the only regressions refixate the repeated word, seems to be a method of comprehending the repeated word, although it may also show the reader confirmed that what he thought he saw was right and decided to go on even though "barge canal" made little sense to him.

In contrast to the confirmation-type repetitions exemplified by Mike's example, other repeated words and phrases are never fixated, even on regression. This is further evidence that repetitions are not necessarily signs of processing the miscued word itself. That is, since traditionally, fixating a word is usually considered evidence of processing that word, *not* fixating it would support the idea that that word is not being actively attended to by the reader. Vera provides an example of a repeated word that does not receive a fixation in Figure 4–7 below:

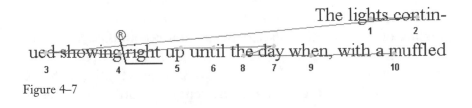

Figure 4–7

Here Vera verbalizes "right," fixates UP, fixates UNTIL and DAY, regresses to THE, then verbalizes "right" again. She is not spending time processing the word *right* but is processing the text after it. There is an indication of tentativeness, as if a prediction has been disconfirmed. Repeating the word allows Vera to return to a known area of the text before continuing to construct her parallel text. The following pattern, which we'll call a "regression sandwich," is an overwhelmingly prevalent pattern, existing in 96 percent of the repetition miscues in a recent study (Paulson 2000):

first utterance ⟶ regressive fixation sequence ⟶
second utterance ⟶ forward fixation sequence

In the following excerpt (Figure 4–8), Astor provides another example:

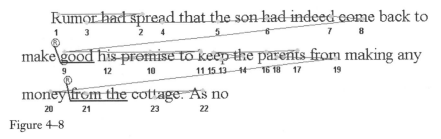

Figure 4–8

The eye movement and miscue time course of these two repetitions are very similar to Vera's. Astor fixates GOOD, verbalizes "good," fixates PROMISE and KEEP, regresses to HIS, then repeats "good." On the third line, he fixates MONEY, and FROM, verbalizes "from the," fixates the first word in the following sentence, regresses to COTTAGE, then repeats "from the" (note that he never fixates *THE* although he verbally produces it twice). In both of these repetitions, Astor produces the "regression sandwich" combination of fixations and speech found in almost all instances of repetition.

In this sequence, *all* regressive eye movements are produced *before* the repeated word is uttered for the final time, so the very tentative sampling of the text takes place between oral repetitions. As we saw with Astor's examples, the regressive sequence can take place to the right of the repeated word—one or two forward fixations, then a regression or series of regressions. The repeated word thus acts as an anchor for the reader. This is an important concept because the repeated word is sometimes assumed to be a trouble word for the reader when, in fact, these eye movement and miscue analysis data show the reader using that word as a known word. From this known word, the reader anchors himself as he examines a trouble spot, then returns to the known word to resume reading.

After probing an area of the text that doesn't match their predictions, readers can use the oral repetition to attempt that area of difficulty from a springboard of confidence—the repeated word—before diving into the less easy portion of the text. It is similar to the idea of a running start that has been discussed in miscue analysis, in which readers, after encountering an area of the text that gives them problems, return to the beginning of a phrase or sentence that did not present them with difficulty in order to try the problematic area "from the top."

## Summary

In this chapter we combined eye movement recording with miscue analysis in order to add another dimension of data to how we understand reading processes. We provided Tim's oral reading to go along with the eye movement record we have referred to throughout the previous three chapters. Contrary to what we might expect, when readers make oral miscues while reading aloud, they don't skip the word or fail to look at it long enough; the opposite is true. Readers are likely to look right at words they miscue, and for a longer than average duration. We also discussed what happens when readers orally repeat words while reading aloud and what the purpose of that repetition may be. In the next chapter, we again look at Tim as a reader, but this time, we thoroughly explore a new instructional strategy that relies on using a reader's eye movements and miscues through examining how the strategy worked for Tim.

## Extension Questions

1. In addition to miscue analysis, what are some ways to understand how well your students comprehend what they are reading?
2. When readers make oral reading miscues, more often than not they look directly at the word they omit or substitute. Yet, they rarely make an oral reading miscue on words they don't fixate. What in the reading process accounts for this phenomenon?
3. We've discussed some of Tim's specific miscues in this chapter. Look again at the miscues he makes (in Figure 4–3), specifically the insertions of *all* in two places and the omission of *should* in the last sentence. What do those miscues (and his others) tell you about his reading process and *how* he read this passage?
4. Now that you've become familiar with Tim's eye movements and miscues, how would you work with him to help him become a more efficient reader?
5. Based on what we've discussed in this chapter about repetitions, what do you think is going on when you hear your students repeat words as they read aloud? What should you do, if anything, to improve a student's reading if he or she very often repeats words while reading aloud?
6. In this and previous chapters, we discussed some intuitions about reading that readers—we, you, educators, and so on—may hold about reading that turn out to be unsupported by eye movement research. Some would say that this is the reason research is done: to examine our preconceived notions to see if they stand up under

scrutiny. Others would say that anything that doesn't support intuitive understandings about reading must be wrong. Where do you come down on this debate—is there room for research in reading, or do we already know everything we need to know?

## Eye Movement Links to Reading Instruction

By examining what readers' eyes do when they miscue or when they orally repeat portions of text, we are better informed about what strategies they use to successfully make sense of text. One very important observation that comes out of the combination of eye movement and miscue analyses (EMMA) is the amount of eye movement activity that takes place when readers pause during oral reading. One clear example of this is what we've shown readers do in the silence between oral repetitions, where they make at least one regressive sequence before continuing with their oral reading. Without an eye tracker, it's difficult to tell exactly what a reader is working on when she pauses during oral reading, but the research has shown us that this is decidedly not a time of inactivity. When readers are silent, their eye movements show continued activity as they make sense of text.

### Wait Time: An Approach

A simple but very useful strategy that is supported by our EMMA research is to provide wait time for readers who are reading text aloud. With young readers we are often tempted to jump in and supply the next word when the student pauses. By looking at various eye movement examples, however, we see that readers are working very hard during these pauses. Remember our examples in Chapter 3 when Victoria took a few seconds to reread a section of text around the word *touted* and when Andrea paused to look back at the words *Mary Lopez*, which were printed in italics? A pause does not necessarily mean that a reader is stuck on the next word. Teachers can help students by providing wait time and by expecting that other students in the class will also respect this silent time when the reader is using strategies to work through the text.

In a recent presentation, Yetta Goodman repeated a metaphor—the "football metaphor"—used frequently by Dorothy Watson that may illustrate our point. In football practice, if the coach gets on the field too often, the players won't learn how to play without him once it's game time. Since the coach often knows more about the game than his players, he naturally wants to get out on the field and help them out, but the players need to go through the process of learning how to play, just as their coach once did. So the coach needs to learn to stay on the sidelines when appropriate—just as the teacher needs to know when to let readers read and figure things out for themselves. Many educators believe thirty seconds is a good general amount of time to wait before offering assistance to the reader.

## Four Strategies

Many teachers we have shared these data with are surprised to see that when readers miscue, they tend to have spent quite a bit of time looking right at the portion of text they miscued. A simple strategy for educators based on this information is to avoid telling students to look at the word when they produce a miscue. As we discussed in this chapter, EMMA research shows that they probably have looked at the word, and for quite awhile! Instead, it is helpful to acknowledge the strategies readers are using to make sense of text and to help the readers themselves become aware of what strategies they use. Together, teachers and students can determine which strategies are most helpful. As discussed in Chapter 3, the Strategy Ruler is one tool that can be used to help accomplish this. In the following section, we describe four more strategies for helping readers make sense of text and become aware of their reading process and strategies.

## Adoption Day at the Animal Shelter

This strategy helps engage students in thought and discussion about the role of prediction in reading. Students will discuss how readers can miscue even when they are looking right at the words in a text. They will then explore their own process of making predictions during reading as they read an adaptation of Hazelwood's *Day at the Zoo* (Goodman, Watson, and Burke 1996, 81), called "Adoption Day at the Animal Shelter" (adapted by Ann Hinkle).

**Preparation:** Make an overhead of Miscues on Pack (Figure 4–9) and "Adoption Day at the Animal Shelter." (Full-size reproducibles of these can be found at www.heinemann.com/paulsonfreeman.)

### Adoption Day at the Animal Shelter

The day was rainy and cold—a good day to be inside at the animal shelter. Meowing and barking filled the rooms.

"Look at that cute little one," said Beth.

"Quick, try and get his attention, maybe he'll do something cute," shouted Jason.

"Okay. Oh, he's looking right at us! Sometimes they act just like cute little people!"

"He's coming closer. Is he interested? Does he like us? What should I do?"

"The doors are opening. Others are coming in! Last one down is a scaredy-cat!" Beth challenged as she leaped to the floor from the shelf at the top of the cage.

"Oh, Beth, wait for me," pleaded Jason. "Adoption Day at the animal shelter is the very best time of the week. I hope somebody picks us!"

**Procedure:** Place Miscues on Pack on the overhead. Explain to your students that these three readers all made the same miscue when they read this section of text. Because their eye movements were recorded as they read aloud, we can see that all three readers looked right at the word PACK but read *backpack* aloud. Ask the class how it is possible for these readers to have looked right at PACK and read *backpack*. Discuss with students the strong role our predictions play in reading.

Next, place "Adoption Day at the Animal Shelter" on the overhead and ask students to read the story to themselves quietly. Invite students to turn to a neighbor when they are done reading and retell the story. They should discuss anything that might have been tricky about the story. During these discussions, students will begin to talk about the surprise ending to the text. Ask the class what they predicted Beth and

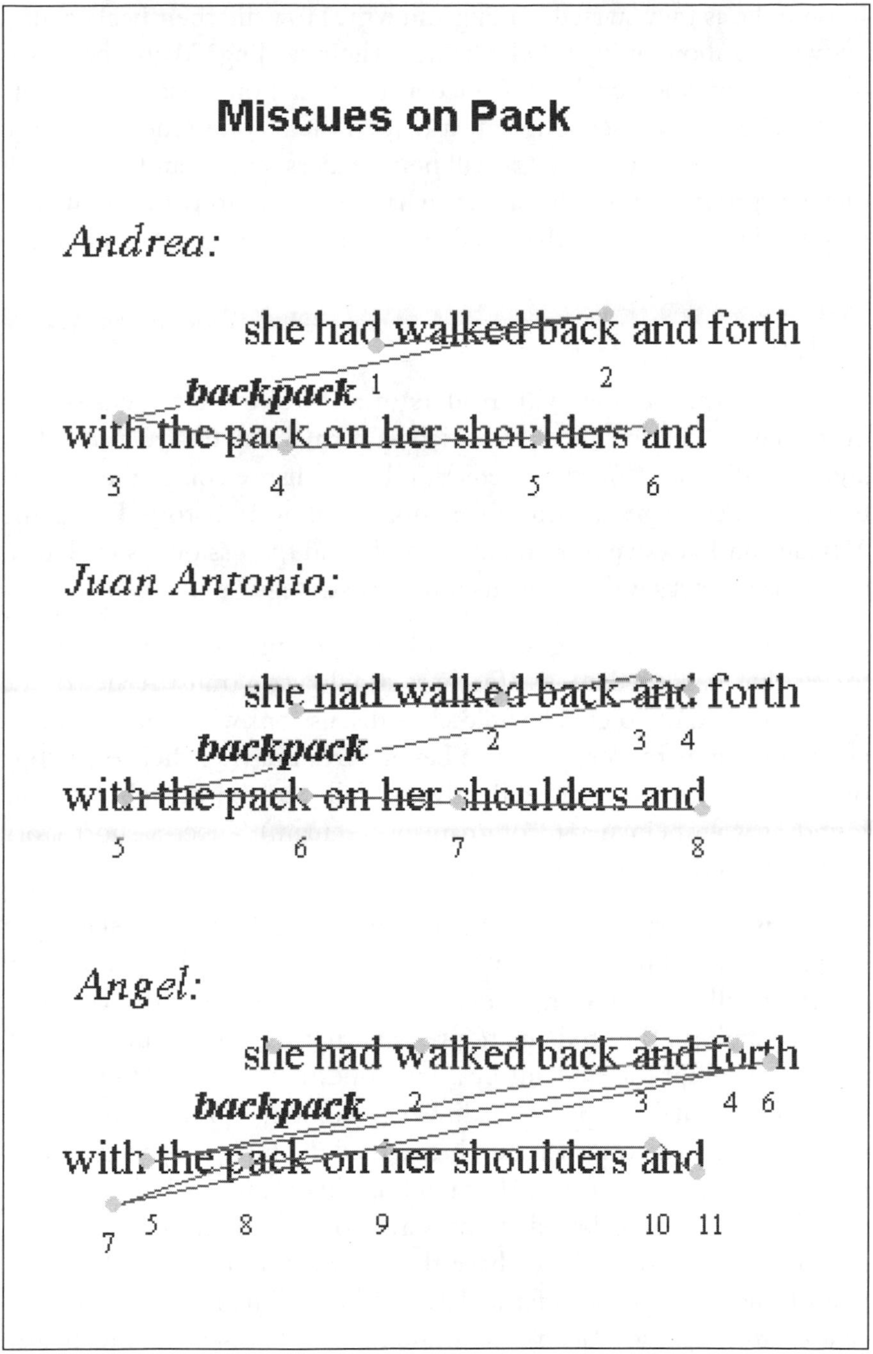

# Miscues on Pack

*Andrea:*

she had walked back and forth

***backpack*** 1                                    2

with the pack on her shoulders and

3            4                    5        6

*Juan Antonio:*

she had walked back and forth

***backpack*** 2                        3   4

with the pack on her shoulders and

5            6            7                    8

*Angel:*

she had walked back and forth

***backpack*** 2                            3        4  6

with the pack on her shoulders and

7   5        8            9                        10   11

Figure 4–9

Jason to be as they started reading and why. How did their background knowledge about animal shelters affect their reading? Were their predictions confirmed or disconfirmed as they read on? Ask the students to talk about which sections of text helped them comprehend who the characters were. This strategy will help readers understand how much our background knowledge affects what we expect to read. It will also help readers understand that prediction plays an important role in the reading process.

## *Prediction Guide*

This guide can be used with readers of all ages to help focus on the process of prediction and is essentially a formal way to structure a talk about prediction. Effective prediction helps ensure comprehension of text and encourages a focus on comprehending the story. Using the Miscues on Pack eye movement example and discussion, as explained previously, works well as a lead-in to this strategy.

**Preparation:** For all ages, you will need a large board and markers for writing class predictions. Teachers should use a transparency of the Prediction Guide to guide whole-class discussions with younger readers, while older readers may also benefit from having their own copy of the guide to use independently. (A full-size reproducible can be found at www.heinemann.com/paulsonfreeman.) Select a short story that your students have not read.

**Procedure:** Explain to your students that you will be sharing a strategy that will help them with their reading by focusing on predicting what will come next in a story. Read the title of the story you have selected and ask the students to predict what the story will be about. You may prompt the students by asking questions such as Who will be in it? or Will it be happy or sad? Write students' predictions on the board or overhead transparency. Next, read the first two paragraphs of the story aloud to the class. After reading this section, ask the students to refine their original predictions. Cross out or add to the list of predictions on the board. Next, have the students think about the information that they know so far and ask: What will happen next? Where is the story going? Again, list students' predictions on the board. Continue this pattern as you read the story to the class. Students

## Prediction Guide

*Read the* title *and predict what the story will be about. Who will be in it? Will it be happy or sad?*

WRITE YOUR PREDICTIONS HERE:

*Read the first* two *paragraphs and stop. Think about the information that you know so far. What will happen next? Where is the story going?*

WRITE YOUR PREDICTIONS HERE:

Continue *to stop reading after every two to four paragraphs and make predictions about what will happen next.*

*Don't forget to* continually ask yourself *if your predictions were accurate or if the story is going in a totally different direction.*

*It's not necessary to continue to write down your predictions after every two to four paragraphs unless you find that you forget your predictions or have trouble articulating them.*

should focus on whether their predictions were accurate after you have read each section.

Ask students to share how this activity was helpful for understanding the story. For older students, provide copies of the Prediction Guide and encourage them to use the guide as they read independently. Explain that the point of the guide is not to spend time writing down predictions, but to get in the habit of paying attention to what has happened in the story and always guessing what will happen next in the story.

## Retrospective Miscue Analysis

One of the most effective ways to help students understand the reading process is to have them reflect on the miscues that they make as they read. This strategy is called Retrospective Miscue Analysis, or RMA (Goodman and Marek 1996b).

**Preparation:** Make an overhead of Miscues on Pack. Select a book for the students you will be working with that is a little more difficult than what they usually read independently. Make an enlarged photocopy or typescript of the story so that there is room for you to write in miscues. You will also need a tape recorder with a good microphone and a tape.

**Procedure:** Begin with a discussion of the Miscues on Pack overhead. Have students talk about why they think all three of these readers made the same miscue. Ask your students why they think these readers did not go back and correct their miscues. Were these good miscues? If reading is making meaning of text, did these readers make an *error* when they read "backpack"?

Next, tape-record a student reading the text you have preselected. Later, listen to the tape and record the miscues you hear on your copy of the text. Read through your work and select a couple of miscues that were good miscues. Find those sections on the tape. Next, meet with the student a second time. Have a copy of the text for the student. Ask the student to listen to her reading and to stop the tape when she hears something that is different than what she sees on the page. To build the student's confidence, have her begin at a section where she has produced a good miscue. Listening and discussing a good miscue that makes sense could help a student realize that an *error* isn't necessarily *bad*, because getting the meaning is more important than getting all of the words right. When the student comes to miscues that do not make sense, you can remind her of the importance of reading for meaning.

In general, the RMA proceeds on a two-day cycle. On day one, the reader is audiotaped while reading a text aloud and retelling the text. After that session, in preparation for the second session, the instructor listens to the tape, marks and codes the miscues the reader made, and holistically assesses the retelling. The instructor then plans which miscues to discuss during the RMA session on the subsequent day. During the RMA session—day two of the RMA cycle—the instructor uses two tape recorders, one to play the reader's oral reading from the day before and one to tape-record the RMA session itself. Using questions like "Does the miscue make sense?" and "Did the miscue affect your understanding of the story?" as discussion prompts, the instructor and reader discuss the reader's reading, retelling, and miscues in a way that engenders an understanding of the reader's reading and the reading process in general. (More specific question guides are provided in the next chapter.) At the end of the RMA session, the reader may read another text for use in a subsequent RMA session.

For a complete how-to book on RMA, see Goodman and Marek (1996a). RMA has been conducted successfully with students as young as second grade. As students engage in RMA, they begin to realize that reading always needs to make sense. In the next chapter, we discuss in detail an adaptation of RMA that involves students discussing their eye movements as well as their miscues.

# Chapter 5

## Helping Students Become Better Readers: Working with Tim

*I*n the previous chapters we've discussed eye movement research and what it demonstrates about reading processes. In each chapter we have described instructional strategies that are based on what eye movements reveal about the reading process. We think of these strategies as pedagogical outcomes of eye movement research— the links to instructional strategies that are related to understandings of the reading process provided by eye movements. The purpose of this chapter is to introduce and model a new instructional strategy that has an even more direct link between eye movements and instruction, which is done after a student has had an assessment with an eye tracker. The strategy uses a reader's own eye movements as the basis for a series of individualized reading lessons. As we mentioned in the introduction, it is not uncommon for schools or districts to own eye-tracking assessment equipment, as many units are equal in price to other reading assessment packages.

We've referred back to Tim's example several times as an anchor for discussions about eye movements in this book. Now that we have an Eye Movement Miscue Analysis record of Tim's reading, how can we help Tim become a better reader?

## Eye Movements as Assessment

Despite some proprietary organizations' claims to the contrary, eye movements can't tell us how well or poorly a reader comprehends a text. However, there are certain patterns of eye movements that indicate the reader has difficulty with a portion of the text—patterns such as multiple fixations within a word, a series of regressions (right-to-left fixations in English texts), longer than average fixation durations, or a combination of these. The absence of these patterns, while not able to demonstrate comprehension, suggests that the reader did not have undue trouble with that portion of the text (Paulson and Henry 2002).

More informative than simply looking at an eye movement record of a reader's reading is comparing that record with his oral reading of the same text, by recording the reader's eye movements while he reads aloud. This enables an analysis of the reader's eye movements to be combined with a miscue analysis of his oral reading and has been termed Eye Movement Miscue Analysis (EMMA) in a recent series of publications (Paulson 2000, 2002; Duckett 2001, 2002; Freeman 2001). This analysis takes into account information about where the reader looked and what the reader read aloud and produces a powerful window on the reading process.

More pedagogically significant than merely using eye movements as part of an assessment package, however, is using EMMA *with* the student as an instructional strategy. In the same way that a student's miscues can be explored with him through Retrospective Miscue Analysis (RMA), a student's eye movements and miscues can be analyzed and discussed through an approach termed Retrospective Eye Movement Miscue Analysis (REMMA).

## Retrospective Eye Movement Miscue Analysis

The theoretical and pedagogical basis for REMMA is Retrospective Miscue Analysis. As we discussed briefly in the previous chapter, RMA is a one-on-one instructional strategy that makes use of a reader's own miscues to explore the reading process (Goodman and Marek 1996b). The essence of RMA is a collaborative discussion between the reader and instructor that explores the reader's miscues with a view toward improving the reader's reading. Specifically, RMA involves engaging a reader in discussing particular excerpts of the oral reading that were tape-recorded for miscue analysis purposes. Reader miscues are highlighted as a means of discussing the reader's strategies and knowledge of language. The goals of RMA are twofold: (1) to allow readers to discuss their own reading process to better understand and value the complex processes of reading and thereby revalue themselves as readers and learners and (2) to allow the instructor (or teacher-researcher) to investigate with the readers their reading strategies and thereby confirm understandings held about reading and/or come to greater understandings about reading processes (Goodman and Marek 1996b).

Procedures for RMA sessions vary according to the situation and reader. In general, they consist of audiotaping a reader reading aloud a complete text that is new to her, then performing miscue analysis on that reading. In a subsequent session, the reader and instructor listen to the tape of the reading while following along on a marked or unmarked typescript of the text. As touched on briefly at the end of Chapter 4, the reader and instructor discuss the reader's miscues, often utilizing open-ended questions like the following (Goodman and Marek 1996b, 45):

1. Does the miscue make sense?
2. Does the miscue sound like language?
3. a. Was the miscue corrected?
   b. Should it have been?

*If the answer to questions 1 and 3a was no, then ask:*
4. Does the miscue look like what was on the page?
5. Does the miscue sound like what was on the page?

*For all miscues, ask:*
6. Why do you think you made this miscue?
7. Did that miscue affect your understanding of the text?

The discussion is geared toward understanding why certain miscues were made, what they reveal about the reader and reading in general, and how this knowledge can lead to gains in reading. This same basic format is followed for REMMA sessions, with the addition of the following questions:

1. What area of the text looks like you had an easy time reading it? Which area looks like it was more difficult? What's the difference?
2. What were you looking at in this section?
3. Describe your eye movements here. Do you see any patterns?

4. Why do you think you looked at this part again/two times/etc.?
5. What were you looking at while you made that miscue?
6. What did you look at while you were correcting that miscue?

As with general RMA, REMMA questions are not asked in a pre-determined order but are used as guidelines for shaping the discussion within a session. The framework of each REMMA session is more structured because of the order in which the readings must be recorded, analyzed, then discussed. A typical session follows:

1. Session 1: first meeting with the student
   a. Teacher and students discuss student's feelings about and definitions of reading. The Burke Interview (Goodman, Watson, and Burke 1987) or Burke Interview Modified for Older Readers (BIMOR) is a good guide for this discussion (see Goodman and Marek 1996a for an example).
   b. Student reads a text aloud while being eye tracked and tape-recorded.
   c. Student retells the text when finished reading.

2. Preparation for the next session
   a. Teacher marks typescript and codes miscues from previous session.
   b. Teacher overlays plot of eye movements on a clean (no miscue marks) typescript.
   c. Teacher plans next session: makes notes about which miscues and/or eye movements to begin discussing.

3. Next session
   a. Teacher gives student a typescript that has her eye movements overlaid on it and explains that student and teacher will discuss her reading and eye movements.
   b. Teacher can preselect areas of the text to discuss, or student can listen to a recording of her oral reading and decide what sections to focus on.
   c. Student and teacher discuss miscues and eye movements using the aforementioned questions as guides.

4. Same or subsequent session: Student reads another text for a REMMA discussion at a later session.

The goal of REMMA sessions is to engage the reader in a discussion about her reading in a way that is natural and comfortable for both instructor and student, so these guidelines are just that—guides that are useful in keeping the discussion moving in a positive direction. Interesting tangents, especially those that are generated by the student, should be followed and related back to the reading discussion as much as possible.

A number of dialogue categories surface regularly in REMMA discussions within the previous guidelines, including critical moment instruction and discovery learning. These and other aspects of REMMA sessions are described in the following sections using examples from two REMMA sessions with Tim.

## Aspects of REMMA Sessions

In the following sections, we describe several aspects of typical REMMA sessions through two sessions with Tim, the teenage reader we've referred to throughout this book. Tim has a low level of confidence in his reading that stems from poor reading test results. He believes that everyone else he knows is a better and faster reader than he is, and he believes good readers understand and remember everything they read. Part of the purpose of REMMA is to explore these parts of his belief system en route to helping him improve his reading ability.

### Beginnings: A Discussion of What Eye Movements and Miscues Are

An introduction to the topics of discussion—the reader's eye movements and miscues—is usually necessary only at the beginning of the first session. Yet it is important that the reader becomes comfortable with these concepts. You may want to explain that you're interested in discussing where the reader looked and what he said and go from there. This is also a good opportunity to set up the routine of the session, to demonstrate that you're interested in hearing the reader talk about his ideas of what's going on. The following short exchange shows the instructor, Eric, demonstrating how to read the eye movement overlay and encouraging the reader, Tim, to jump right in and describe what he sees:

ERIC: Let's look at the eye movements. . . . Here are the dots where you stopped. The lines connect them, so you looked at the title, then went to AGE OF, then went back there, then went back up with one fixation there, went there, and here's where you said "just."

TIM: Yeah [laughs].

ERIC: Tell me what was going on right there—I mean, what your eyes were doing in that area.

After a brief introduction in reading eye movement overlays and in miscue terminology, encourage the reader to talk about both eye movements and miscues in any way he feels comfortable.

## Reader's Overall Impressions

An important beginning to each session is an open-ended question about the reader's impression of his reading. This is important not only as a way to warm up and begin the session but also as a way to identify what some of the themes of the session may be. The reader can give his overall impression in a few ways, including listening to a tape of his reading in its entirety while following along on a blank typescript and then immediately talking about his impressions or recalling his impressions from the session in which he first read the text. In Tim's first session, he watched a video of his reading (the eye-tracking system used produces a video of the text with a cursor that represents the student's eye movements moving in real time across the lines of text, while his oral reading is simultaneously produced) and summed up his impressions by saying, "Listening to it, I was incredibly slow. And real choppy." At the beginning of the second session, instead of watching the videotape in order to hear his oral reading, Tim looked at his eye movements by examining a printout of the texts he read on which his eye movements were overlaid. He looked at two versions: one with the eye fixations shown as same-size circles and one with the eye movements shown as variable-size circles, depending on how long the duration of each eye movement was (larger circle equals longer duration, smaller circle equals shorter duration). Excerpts from these two versions are shown in Figures 5–1 and 5–2 below.

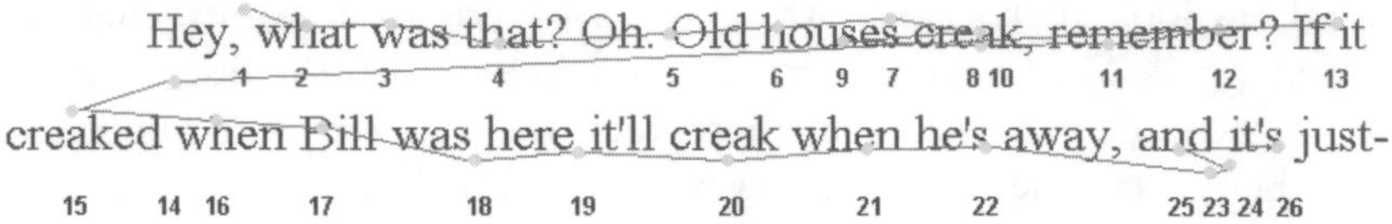
Hey, what was that? Oh. Old houses creak, remember? If it
1 2 3 4 5 6 9 7 8 10 11 12 13
creaked when Bill was here it'll creak when he's away, and it's just-
15 14 16 17 18 19 20 21 22 25 23 24 26

Figure 5–1

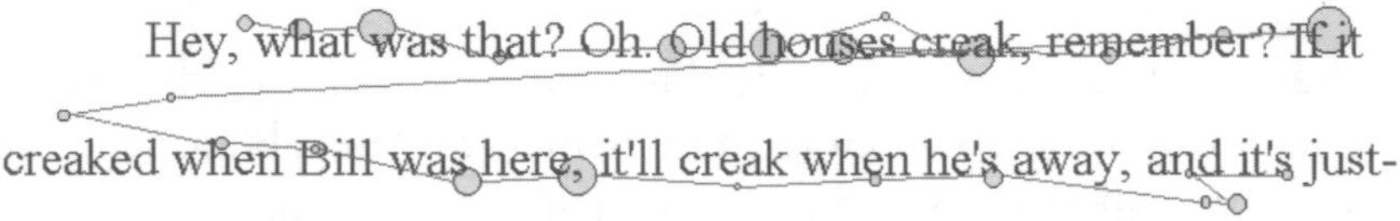
Hey, what was that? Oh. Old houses creak, remember? If it
creaked when Bill was here, it'll creak when he's away, and it's just-

Figure 5–2

Because the eye movement graphics can obscure the words on the typescript, when discussing these readings, Tim and Eric would often refer to a clean manuscript. Based on his eye movements, Tim expressed his overall impression of his reading of the second passage.

TIM: Well, more so than yesterday, I notice just kind of the smoothness from line to line, it doesn't look like I went back too many times, looking at this one. But then, the amount of time spent on each fixation seems like it's still a little long. So you can tell by this one [variable-size printout] that it's still a little choppy.

Tim's overall impressions of his reading as being slow and choppy became a recurring theme of both of these sessions.

## *Critical Moment Teaching*

Critical moment teaching is at the heart of REMMA dialogues. Also called teachable moments, critical moment teaching is the broaching and discussing of important information at a time when the student appears interested and ready to grapple with specific new concepts. It is the opposite of a scripted, "canned" lesson in which information is presented to students regardless of their interest or readiness. Often, critical moment teaching is marked by a student raising a point or question and the teacher using that opportunity to discuss that specific point and connect it to larger issues. For example, in the complex process that is reading, readers will sometimes look directly at a word that they miscue while visually skipping a word that they read aloud verbatim, as we discussed in Chapter 4. This phenomenon is an excellent jumping-off point for discussions about the reading process but only if discussed in a critical moment format, that is, as it is discovered in the reading. The exchange below, from Tim's first session, illustrates the critical moment approach of discussing an important concept. In his oral reading, he substituted the word *a* for the text item *the*, reading " . . . polenta recently made an appearance on a grand stage . . . ."

An Italian peasant food

whose primary virtue has traditionally been that it would stick to

farmers' ribs during winter, polenta recently made an appearance
   *a*
on the grand stage of American cuisine.

Figure 5–3

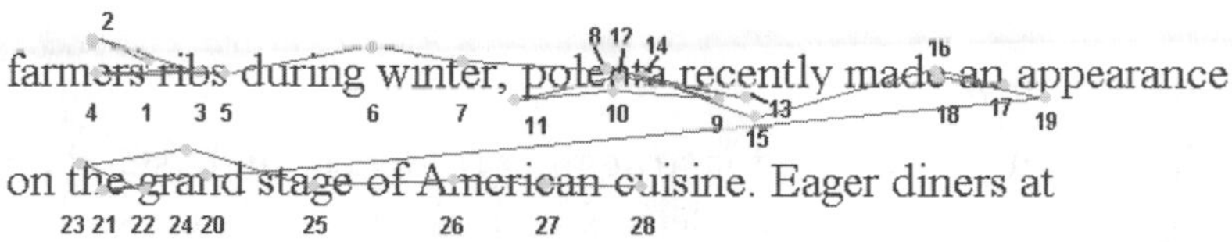

farmers' ribs during winter, polenta recently made an appearance
on the grand stage of American cuisine. Eager diners at

Figure 5–4

ERIC: What other miscues do you find? Let's listen to it again. [*Eric plays tape*]

TIM: I didn't say "the."

ERIC: Okay, what did you say there instead?

TIM: "On a," I think—"on a grand stage . . . ."

ERIC: Now isn't that interesting, 'cause look at these two words [*on* and *the*]. Which one has the fixations?

TIM: *The.*

ERIC: Which one does not have fixations?

TIM: *On.*

ERIC: Which one did you miscue?

TIM: *The.* [laughs]

ERIC: Isn't that interesting?

TIM: Yeah.

ERIC: Let's see, you started on that word, then went back to *the* back there, and back again, then finally continued going on. So what does that tell you? I think that's a little interesting right there, that you skip words, everybody does, when they're reading, but in the skipped word, you said it correctly, but the word right next to it that you looked right at, that's the one you miscued. What can explain that?

TIM: I don't know, but they're both really short, common words—*on* and *the*. Sometimes for *on* I find myself saying "one" occasionally. I don't know—I hit *grand* first, then went to *the*—maybe that's it . . . 'cause I went to *grand* first, it's almost like I stopped on the *a*, so maybe that's where the source of the *a* came from, 'cause *the* doesn't look anything like *a*.

Here, Tim begins to analyze different ways that he uses text information to construct meaning. By broaching the subject of "sometimes one *looks* but doesn't *see*" while looking at and discussing an example of himself doing just that, he generates a genuine interest in analyzing his reading process. It is in this way that REMMA procedures encourage critical moment teaching.

## Discovery Learning

One important perspective for struggling readers to understand is that reading is not simply adding letters to make words, words to make sentences, sentences to make paragraphs, and so on, but also involves constructing meaning using the text and their own minds. While the instructor could simply tell the student this, it wouldn't have much effect; as Knowles, Holton, and Swanson (1998) point out, learners need to discover for *themselves* the nature of the thing they are learning. In the exchange below, Tim and Eric explore a series of backward and forward eye movements surrounding a miscue he made (see Figure 5–5 and 5–6 below). As the miscue markings indicate, he said, "It used to be the other way around—the lower class wanted the upper class had—the lower classes wanted what the upper classes had."

It used to be the other
©      *class*      *class*
way around—the lower classes wanted what the upper classes had.

Figure 5–5

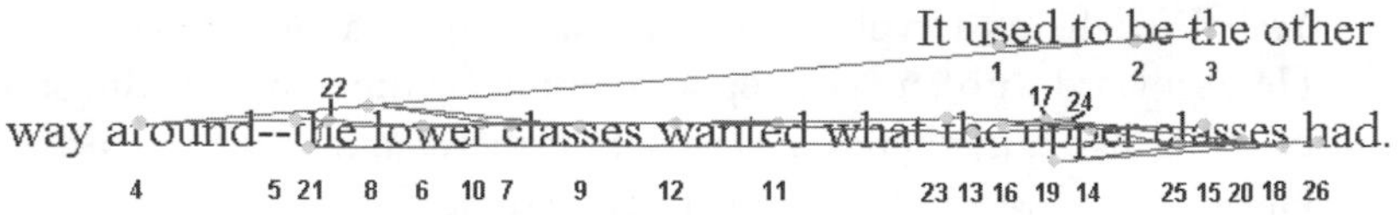
It used to be the other
1 2 3
22
17 24
way around--the lower classes wanted what the upper classes had.
4 5 21 8 6 10 7 9 12 11 23 13 16 19 14 25 15 20 18 26

Figure 5–6

ERIC: [*on a new miscue*] It looks like you went here . . . and then down to this line, like you were going to go on, decided something looked weird, then came back up here, and went back and forth.

TIM: Yeah. I guess, 'cause the most frequent motion is just to go on. Then I realized, computed, that it didn't make sense, and went back and fixed it.

ERIC: How did you fix it? I mean, what was the missing word?

TIM: *What.*

ERIC: So tell me about the eye movements around *what* there.

TIM: I didn't hit *what* once!

ERIC: Never looked at it! Isn't that interesting?

TIM: Yeah!

ERIC: So maybe you could say you didn't look at it so you didn't see it the first time, and missed it, but how did you know to put it in if you never looked at it?

TIM: I guess kind of like fill in the blank, sort of, I just made the connection and made it make sense with what came after it.

Tim reasons that he didn't need to see the word he initially omitted when he subsequently corrected himself because he mentally filled in the blank, "made the connection and made it make sense." Of course, this is what the instructor hopes will happen: that Tim will focus on meaning as he reads. But to tell him that without letting him discover his strength in that area on his own would not have the same impact.

In a similar way, Tim makes a breakthrough in his thinking about what makes a text hard in the exchange below. Because Tim had told Eric earlier that the harder the words were, the slower he read, Eric asked him to look at places in the story he had just read (Figure 5–7 below) to identify places where he spent long periods of time.

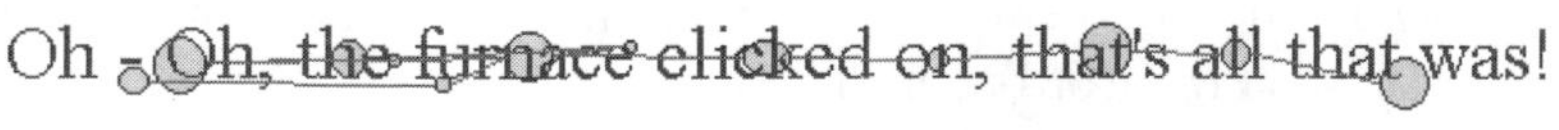
Oh - Oh, the furnace clicked on, that's all that was!

Figure 5–7

TIM: Yeah. Well, here's a hyphenated word, and I spent a lot of time on that. Here's a word with an apostrophe, spent more time on that. But some of them, like *was*, there's a big fixation there, and that's a word I've known since I was in first grade or something. Umm . . .

ERIC: So is it just the word, or is it . . .

TIM: I guess what comes before the word. Like if the word seems like it's a word maybe that I predicted, it'll be a smaller fixation, but if my mind was thinking another word, maybe the fixation would be bigger, trying to replace the word that's really there for the word my mind put there.

When Tim realizes here that words are only as difficult as the context they're in, he's prepared himself for real growth in reading comprehension. REMMA allows him to discover for himself what he does as a reader and presents him with an opportunity to explore that process to better understand how reading happens.

## Formalizing Concepts

The second R of the classic study strategy SQ3R is *recite*—after surveying a chapter, making questions about the headings, and then reading it, SQ3R strategy maintains that the student then summarize what he has read in some fashion. This is no accident; students are more aware of what they've learned if given an opportunity to review and recite (Sotiriou 2002). For REMMA purposes, this involves time at the end of each session to allow the instructor and student to recap and, if desired, to further some concepts. In this excerpt from our second session, Tim again raises the issue of skipping words and what that has to do with reading.

ERIC: Anything you didn't expect?

TIM: I really didn't expect to skip words.

ERIC: With your eyes?

TIM: Yeah, with your eyes.

ERIC: Okay.

TIM: So, that was kind of interesting, but . . .

ERIC: How is it possible that you can skip words but still say them? And read them and understand them?

TIM: Your mind puts them into the context, and just kind of, it guesses, really, what the word's gonna be.

ERIC: Random guess?

TIM: No. [laughs] With what you already know about the subject and what you've already read so far.

In the last few lines of this excerpt, Tim articulates an important aspect of the reading process and demonstrates his understanding of how he reads and makes sense of the text.

### Revaluing Reading and Reader

In the "overall impressions" stage of the beginning of both of our sessions, Tim remarked that his reading sounded and looked slow and choppy. Eric wanted to examine that strong impression of his, so they looked at the following part of one of the texts he'd read:

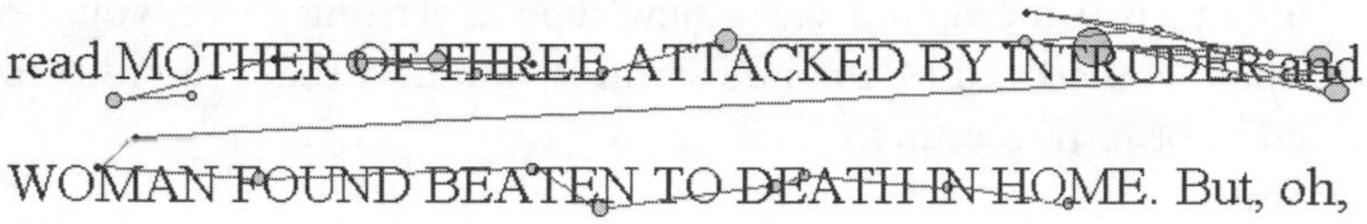

read MOTHER OF THREE ATTACKED BY INTRUDER and

WOMAN FOUND BEATEN TO DEATH IN HOME. But, oh,

Figure 5–8

In this section, the narrator of the story is recounting her reading of two headlines in the newspaper, signified in the text by all capitals. Tim made more regressive eye movements on the first headline, as well as spending a longer time on it. The discussion about that section revolved around the differences in his eye movements on the two newspaper headlines:

ERIC: So what about the capital letters there? What do those signify?

TIM: That it was a passage from the paper that she had read, like a heading, I think.

ERIC: I agree. What makes it sound like a heading?

TIM: Kind of pulls you into the reading, almost, makes you want to read more, like a title or something.

ERIC: Is the language different at all, in titles? Like they put it in caps here, and I think that was partly to show you it was something different, but if it weren't in caps, would you have found the wording a little bit strange?

TIM: Yeah. 'Cause "mother of three attacked by intruder" and "woman found beaten to death in home"—it's kind of a different form of writing.

ERIC: Describe the two, what you did with your eyes on the . . . first heading and the second heading.

TIM: The first one, they were a little bigger circles than the second one—longer time spent [on the first heading]. Then the real big one on *intruder* and then I kind of got the gist of what was going on, and for the second one, they were all pretty small. The first one kind of took me by surprise, she was talking about the comics up there, so I guess I should have made the connection it was a paper, but . . .

ERIC: Well, you didn't expect to *read* a headline, though.

TIM: Yeah. True. Right.

ERIC: The first heading you've got back-and-forth regressions, and the fixations are longer. The second one, it pretty much goes left to right, except for one, and the fixations are smaller. I agree, you're getting used to it. I mean, you saw a new type of writing there, you looked where you needed to, to understand it, and next time, you're ready to go—got it. Interesting.

TIM: Yeah.

In this exchange, Eric and Tim begin to agree that Tim's reading isn't slow and choppy all the time; in fact, there's a reason it appears slow and choppy in spots. He slows down and thoroughly examines aspects of the text that are new or unfamiliar, and then, when he has assimilated that information, he speeds back up again. The result is that he reads efficiently—slowing down when he needs to and speeding up when he can. All Tim was aware of before was that he was slow, but examining the two headlines in the text demonstrated that his reading is not always slow and choppy, and that when it is, it is for a reason.

## Summary

In this chapter we described a new reading strategy that uses a reader's own eye movement record as the basis for a series of strategy lessons. Because you have likely become familiar with Tim's excerpts that we have provided throughout this book, we chose to focus on Tim's REMMA sessions with Eric and detail how he responded to them.

Why not simply tell students what reading strategies to use? Why show them their eye movements at all? The reason is this basic educational premise: if they are allowed to share in the learning experience, they are more likely to understand the reading process and their own specific reading strengths and challenges. The more they know about how they read, the more they are empowered to improve their reading.

But there is another important aspect of what REMMA can offer: the opportunity for students to revalue themselves as readers. Revaluing, as with Retrospective Miscue Analysis, involves discussions revolving around the qualitative nature of the student's reading. Many readers, like Tim, see few, if any, strengths in their reading abilities. REMMA discussions present opportunities to explore previously unnoticed strengths with the reader, which can result in greater confidence. As Van Der Kamp (1992) reminds us, "effective learning is linked to an individual's self-concept and self-evaluation as a learner" (195). Retrospective Eye Movement Miscue Analysis can be an important part of a reader's growth in understanding reading and in valuing himself as a reader.

# Chapter 6

## Eye Movement Research Supports Constructivist Theories of Reading

*T*hrough references to eye movement research and examinations of actual eye movement records, we have focused on what eye movements tell us about how reading works. While we've introduced (and in some cases reintroduced) strategies based on what eye movements show us readers do while reading, we haven't yet tied this research to any particular reading philosophies or programs. In part, that's logistical—an up-front philosophical statement is not always the best way to construct knowledge, particularly because there are few reading approaches that do not carry with them some negative baggage. But the primary reason we did not begin this book with a statement of our educational philosophy is precisely because, as we implied in the previous sentence, we believe knowledge is constructed, not simply transmitted. By examining the eye movement evidence in this book, and by conducting your own mini-research on the examples provided, we hope your conclusions about the reading process parallel our own. In this chapter we'll review some of what we've presented and connect those findings to an educational perspective.

*Readers sample the text.*

In contrast to claims made by proponents of some theories of reading, readers do not fixate on every letter or every word in a text. On the contrary, readers fixate between one-half and three-quarters of the words in a given text. As we have discussed, this is important, since the area of vision that is in focus is relatively small, and to see a word physiologically, it is necessary to fixate it. This simple fact alone helps us understand that reading cannot be as simple as merely uploading print data to the brain. Based solely on the in-focus data delivered to the reader, the text would be unintelligible. Thus, there must be other interactive processes at work here.

## *Reading is not a process of sequential word recognition.*

The eyes do not plod along regularly through the text but go where the brain directs them in order to gain more text information. The irregular nature of eye movements can at first glance appear haphazard until a closer look reveals that the pattern is to be found not in uniform fixations and fixation durations, but in the reader's quest for meaning. Readers look at content words at around twice the rate that they look at function words, and words or phrases that are ambiguous or otherwise difficult for the reader are fixated longer and more often than other parts of the text. The converse is also true—areas of the text that pose no problems for the reader are fixated to a lesser degree and for a shorter period of time. Readers' eye movements are one indication of reading being an efficient process of meaning making.

## *Both eye movements and miscues, and the relationship between them, are functions of comprehension.*

The relationship between eye movements and miscues is not causal but is an observable aspect of the brain's process of making sense of print. Miscues are not caused by careless or reckless reading, or visually skipping words, but are instead usually fixated, and fixated for a slightly longer period of time on average than the other words in the text. As evidence from the eye movements made relative to miscues demonstrates, readers look at the text and read not what they physiologically fixate on, but what they perceive. Readers read what they think they see. Reading is a perceptual act, not simply the direct input of graphic data.

## *Eye movement research provides an understanding of the reading process upon which can be built reading instructional strategies for classroom use.*

Traditionally, eye movement research has not enjoyed a direct connection between research and practice—that is, few reading curricula have been tested with eye movements. But the contribution eye movement research has made for more than a century to our understanding about how reading works is impressive. It is that understanding of how reading works that enables us to construct strategies for student use—strategies that, in turn, help our students (and us!) understand how we read. We also introduced a powerful new strategy for improving reading effectiveness and efficiency using students' own eye movements, termed Retrospective Eye Movement Miscue Analysis (REMMA).

As we move toward our final summary point, we'll begin discussing eye movements and constructivism. In some ways it seems out of place to discuss eye movement research in the context of constructivist learning theory; after all, the movement of the eyes represents microprocesses at work, and most work involving constructivism concentrates on macroprocesses and wider societal issues—sociocultural contexts in reading and emancipatory literacy, to provide two examples. But that is precisely why it becomes important to discuss eye movements in that context. Often the *type* of research is assumed to show support for a certain educational theory, and eye movement research is a perfect example of that. As we alluded to in the introduction, eye movement research is sometimes assumed by practitioners of holistic teaching approaches to support the "wrong" ideas about literacy. Even ignoring the obvious problems with advocating paying attention to only that research that supports the "right" ideas, the assumption that the research *tool* necessarily predetermines the research *conclusions* is erroneous. In this case, because eye movement research involves examination of split-second attentional foci as inferred by readers' eye movements, one or more assumptions are usually made: (1) eye movement research contributes nothing to our understanding of wider literacy concepts and/or (2) eye movement research provides evidence that runs counter to our understanding of social and cognitive aspects of literacy. As we've noted in a few places throughout this book, several reading theorists make similar assumptions; that is, assumptions about what eye movement *should* say, versus what it *actually* reports. One last example of mistaken assumptions:

> It is important to process every single letter during reading because letter-level cues are the primary means of recognizing words. This conclusion, based on eye movement and related analyses, clashes with the

> whole-language theory of word recognition. . . . [T]his perspective
> [whole language] simply is not supported by outcomes from eye-
> movement research. (Pressley 1998, 43)

Note that one of the first things we tackled in Chapter 1 was that eye
movement research shows that readers do not look at every word,
much less every letter, in a given text. Still, as we pointed out, since
our perception is that we've easily seen every word, it makes intuitive
sense that eye movement research would back that intuition up. Of
course, that's why we do the research—assumptions are not science.
That's a harmless mistake. Or is it? In the previous quote, that
assumption is used to provide evidence against a specific view of the
reading process. Based on our knowledge that the assumption itself is
wrong, we may understand that perhaps the conclusion based on that
assumption is also wrong. This leads us to our final summary point.

### *Eye movement research demonstrates support for models of reading that view reading as a constructivist act.*

Definitions of *constructivism* are, appropriately, varied. Vadeboncoeur
(1997) identifies three major strands of constructivism—psychological,
sociocultural, and emancipatory—and within each, there are specialized
meanings and interpretations of the term (including criticisms of other
strands). But in general educational terms, constructivism is an epistemology, a theory of learning that provides an understanding of knowledge as being constructed by the learner in conjunction with what is
being learned. That is, knowledge is not transmitted but is created. The
roots of constructivist learning theory reach back centuries, at least as
early as Immanuel Kant, the eighteenth-century philosopher concerned
with epistemology. Immanuel Kant's unification of rationalist and
empiricist ideas of knowledge contributes to his view that "knowledge is
only possible because our mind plays an active role, organizing and sys-
tematizing what we experience" (Singer 1983, 117). Kant writes that
only when we use our background knowledge (what he terms *a priori*
knowledge) and what our senses perceive (*a posteriori* knowledge) simultaneously can we "know." He views background knowledge, though *a
priori*, as having its origin in sensory experience; however, while one's
schemata may predispose that person to anticipate and perceive things

a certain way, *a priori* knowledge cannot predict *specific* sensations. He writes: "All cognition, by means of which I am enabled to cognize and determine *a priori* what belongs to empirical cognition, may be called an anticipation. . . . But . . . sensation is just that element in cognition which cannot be at all anticipated" (Kant 1781/1901, 180).

What does this have to do with eye movements? Think about what we looked at and discussed throughout this book; the reader's eyes, the sensory organs as they relate to reading, are responsible for bringing *a posteriori* information from the text to the reader. But the eyes are under the reader's control; they don't simply go from one word to the next to the next to the next. Rather, they go forward, backward, up, down, back to a previous column, skip a word or two, look three or four times at another word, and so on, until the reader can make sense of the ink marks on the page. What the reader needs to find out from the text— where he moves his eyes—is related to what that individual reader already knows: *a priori* information. *A priori* information can be content-related, in terms of knowing a lot or a little about the subject of the reading. But it can also be structure-related, knowledge about the way something is written, its syntax and other textual conventions.

When we combine eye movements with miscue analysis, what we've termed EMMA, we also get a glimpse into the text as the reader understands it—which words were substituted or omitted, where words were inserted, and so on. All of the information we have presented here contradicts a simple behavoristic model of reading. Everything from millisecond-to-millisecond decisions by the reader about where to search for information to how the reader corrects oral reading miscues that impeded comprehension promotes a view of reading that, as Kant expounded in more general epistemological terms, values the individual background and knowledge of the reader.

But by asserting that the reader is important, we are not detracting from the importance of the text during the reading process. Indeed, further reading of Kant's ideas provides epistemological support for the importance of both the knower and the known. His writings indicate that schemata-based expectations cannot predispose one to experience *specific a posteriori* input; putting this in reading terms, our background knowledge cannot predict *exactly* what we will find in that text. We may perceive and interpret what we transact with in the text a certain way, but the text is still a necessary part of the transaction— no amount of background knowledge, schemata, or prediction can completely replace the text.

Kant's ideas, further developed by Dewey and Bentley (1949) in terms of educational theory, and refined in a more specific reading theory sense by Rosenblatt (1978), are the precursors of models of reading described as interactive (e.g., Rumelhart 1994) and transactive (e.g., Goodman 1994). Both the reader and the text are necessary and important variables of the reading process.

If the *text* were the only variable in location and duration of eye movements, we might expect all readers to have the same eye movement patterns when reading a specific text. If the *reader* were the only variable, we would see a single reader's same eye movement pattern across several different texts. Of course, neither of these is the case; eye movements vary between readers, between texts, and between a single reader's reading of the same text at two different times. Eye movement support for this idea is easily traced as far back as 1922, when Buswell reported that "the relative difficulty of the material read or the particular aim of the reader has a direct influence" on the reader's eye movements (22). Even earlier, Huey found that

> the amount that can be read at a reading pause, and consequently the number of necessary pauses and movements per line and page, will vary with the nature of the matter read, with the associative connections existing between the letters, words, etc., and with the reader's familiarity with what is read, the latter enabling any part that may be clear to help into consciousness other parts that are indistinct. (1908, 68)

So the idea that eye movements reflect reader and text variables is hardly new.

Our understanding of the significance of eye movements may be more sophisticated, however. As mentioned in the introduction, observations of the differences between good and poor readers' eye movements has resulted in pedagogical techniques that focused on changing the poor readers' eye movement behavior to more closely match those of the good readers. Since eye movements don't control meaning (instead, the meaning-making process controls eye movements), attempting to improve comprehension by altering readers' eye movement behavior only resulted in stressed-out students.

Instead, it is important for us to understand that readers' eye movements provide a glimpse into their millisecond-by-millisecond reading processes, and what we find is a reflection of the constructive nature of reading. Based on this information, it is clear that pedagogy based on an understanding of reading as a constructive process of meaning making can be effective, both in terms of short-term reading comprehension improvement and lifelong reading habits.

However, as Fosnot (1996, 29) reminds us, "Constructivism is a theory about learning, not a description of teaching. No 'cookbook teaching style' or pat set of instructional techniques can be abstracted from the theory and proposed as a constructivist approach to teaching." The teaching strategies we've outlined here are based on the knowledge that reading is a constructivist act, but there is no such thing as a canned constructivist curriculum. Depending on your purposes, the strategies will assist your and your students' explorations of literacy and can be an important part of how you create knowledge in your classroom. But this is only a piece of the puzzle; Gould (1996) emphasizes that "there are no workbooks or step-by-step guidebooks to a perfect literacy program. To facilitate real learning, a teacher must provide a full-immersion approach to the language arts. Classrooms that are moving in this direction provide relevant, literate talk; real literature; spelling taught in context; and writing that grows out of children's interests, experiences, and expertise" (92). Our hope is that you can integrate your knowledge of what eye movement research has shown you about the reading process into your classroom and that the strategies described here can be part of that process.

# Appendices

*Complete Research Texts*

# Appendix A
## *Wide O-*
### By Elsin Ann Graffam

Maybe I'll put my head under the pillow—no, that's no good. I can imagine him, whoever he is, sneaking up on me. Okay, that does it! I'm going to get up and stay up, put the lights on in the living room, turn on the television.

Oh, I hate going into the dark . . . there! Overhead light on, floor lamp on, TV on, nice and loud. Now I'll just sit down and relax and watch the—

Hey, what was that? Oh. Old houses creak, remember? If it creaked when Bill was here, it'll creak when he's away, and it's just—just something in the house. It's only your imagination, old girl, that's what it is. And the more sleepy you get, the more vivid your imagination will get.

All the doors are locked, right? And all the windows, ditto. Okay, then. So I feel like an idiot, trying to stay up all night. Well, sitting here in the living room is a lot better than doing what I did the last time Bill was away overnight! Locking myself in the bathroom and staying there until dawn, for heaven's sake—

Oh—Oh, the furnace clicked on, that's all that was! Calm down, girl, calm down! The trouble with you is, you read the papers. You should read the comics and stop there. No, I have to read MOTHER OF THREE ATTACKED BY INTRUDER and WOMAN FOUND BEATEN TO DEATH IN HOME. But, oh, they were so close to us! That old lady lived—what was it, only three, four blocks away? But she lived alone, and nobody knows I'm alone tonight. I hope.

What is the matter with me?! I'm acting like a child. Other women live alone—for years, even—and here I have to stay by myself for just one measly little night and I go all to pieces.

Sure seems cold in here! The furnace was on—still is on, in fact. Must be my nerves. I'll go into the kitchen and make myself a nice hot cup of tea. Good idea! Maybe that'll warm me up!

Now, where is that light switch . . . there . . . well, no wonder I'm cold, with the back door standing wide o-

# Appendix B
*Waterford Ghost's Revenge*
By Carroll B. Colby

It's not often that a ghost has a chance to get back at people still alive, but near Waterford, New York, there was supposed to have been one which did just that. The ghost's revenge took place about 1900.

At that time, near the end of a barge canal, there lived a carpenter. He was poor and sick with tuberculosis, but he still worked hard to support his wife and two children with earnings from odd jobs about the village. Unfortunately, his own parents were particularly selfish, cruel and mercenary and demanded that he will them his house and property, which in case of his death would have gone to his wife. This, of course, the carpenter refused to do. Shortly before he did die, he warned his parents that if they did anything to harm his family after he was gone, he would come back and haunt them as long as they themselves lived. He would see to it, he said, that they would never make any profit from his house even if they did get it away from his wife.

As soon as their son had passed away, the parents undertook legal proceedings and did obtain possession of the property, evicting the impoverished wife and youngsters. The house was run down, but usable, and they hoped to rent it rather quickly. So they closed the blinds and waited for a tenant. But no tenant ever rented it, for presently discouraging things began to happen. Some of the neighbors, passing the empty house late at night, soon noticed lights shining between the shuttered windows and from between loose boards along the sides. At first they thought that perhaps the wife had come back and was secretly living there. They had liked the wife, and so did not investigate too carefully.

However, the lights continued to wave about and flicker from within, far too mysteriously for their comfort, and they began to cross the road when they passed that way after dark. Rumor spread that the son had indeed come back to make good his promise to keep the parents from making any money from the cottage. As no one wanted to rent the place it fell more and more into ruin. Even in its last years, when it was completely untenantable, the mysterious lights could be seen still.

The greedy parents nevertheless kept trying to rent or sell the place. No one would listen to them. The lights continued showing right up until the day when, with a muffled crash and a cloud of dry dust, the sagging roof finally fell in and the tottering walls collapsed into the cellar hole. Only then did the lights vanish, never to return.

No one could explain the mysterious lights, but many neighbors felt sure that the Waterford ghost had had its revenge. . . .

© 2003 by Eric J. Paulson and Ann E. Freeman. From *Insight from the Eyes*. Portsmouth, NH: Heinemann.

# Appendix C
*Frugal Gourmets*
By Annette Foglino

In this age of nouvelle richesse, even food is subject to abrupt changes of status. Take polenta, the cornmeal mush often served with beans and sausage floating in it. An Italian peasant food whose primary virtue has traditionally been that it would stick to farmers' ribs during winter, polenta recently made an appearance on the grand stage of American cuisine. Eager diners at Manhattan's Le Cirque 2000 eschewed the restaurant's famous paupiette of black sea bass in Barolo wine sauce for the chance to have a large portion of the yellow gruel dumped directly on their table, just as poor Italian families used to do.

"More and more lower-social-status foods are making their way up the social scale," says nutritional anthropologist Solomon H. Katz, Ph.D., of the University of Pennsylvania. "The same thing is happening with blue corn tortillas. It used to be the other way around—the lower classes wanted what the upper classes had. But the farther up on the social scale we get, the more secure we are in reaching down." For Le Cirque 2000 chef Marc Poidevin, it all makes sense: "They're often totally arbitrary, and never more so than right now in our celebrity culture. Look at Wolfgang Puck. He turned pizza into a high-end food by getting rich and famous people to eat it."

This is not the first time foods have followed the American dream from staple to delicacy. Lobster and salmon were once eaten only by indentured servants. At the turn of the century, caviar was so easy to get that it was given away in bars, like peanuts. Some theorists point to heightened health consciousness to explain the trend, but Betty Fussell, food historian and author of *I Hear America Cooking*, sees it as a perfect illustration of the irrational nature of class distinctions. "When the wealthy have tried everything else, they start expanding to the foods of the poor. They get bored and figure, 'How bad could it be?'"

For those used to expensive food, the experience is a form of gastronomic slumming. "You sit there holding on to this extremely ornate silver spoon," says one recent diner, "and the cooks come and dump gruel on your table. You taste it and then instantly wish you were at a red-and-white-checked table in Italy, with a big peasant family in the background. You almost want to eat with your hands."

Forgotten amid the celebrations of those that reach the top, however, are those foods once considered A-list that have since fallen on hard times. Like parsley. Once a sign of gentility and used as a garnish, parsley has become so declasse that upscale eateries rarely place it on their dishes any more. "If you're served a plate with parsley on it," says Fussell, "you know you're not at Le Cirque."

# Appendix D
*Gesture*

of the whole body, it is evident that what should be first developed is a general physical efficiency.

## VI. GESTURE

### A. Definition

Gesture is that part of the speech code by which communication is accomplished through the visible activity of hands, arms, shoulders, head, and face. The difference between movement and gesture as the terms are used in this book is that gesture is restricted to apply to the speech activity of certain parts of the body, while movement is used to denote more general and total actions such as changes in posture and position. Lively conversation is largely made up of gestures.

Almost any activity of the instruments of gesture may at some time be effective, and, just as in the case of movement, not only gesture but absence of gesture is pretty sure to carry meanings. If hands, arms, head, and face are inert and immobile, they still carry meanings. Moving or motionless, they mean something all the time. No speaker can dodge the problem of gesture any more than he can dodge the problems of posture, movement, clothes, or a clean face.

### B. General Principles of Gesture

There are certain rather definite conventional restrictions which have been placed upon gesture, certain general principles of effectiveness, widely accepted, to be neglected at the speaker's own risk. Let us now consider some of these general principles.

#### 1. *Every Gesture Should be of the Whole Body*

Gesture is not something to be added on to speech; it is an integral part of speech and should be trained into the total activity of the whole body. In gesture no joint or muscle liveth unto itself alone. All our gestures are affected by what the *basic* muscles do—those of the back, trunk, arms, legs, and neck. These muscles are the earliest to be mastered in infancy and their habits are most easily understood as speech signs, and such activity makes or mars the effect produced by the more delicate muscles of the hands and face. Very often the cause of awkwardness in the wrist or elbow may be found at the ankle, knee, or hip. The stiff hand positions of boys and girls are almost always the results of tensions in the larger muscles of the body. A gesture seldom is effective unless it originates in and is an integral part of a *general attitude or activity of the body.*

## *2. Gestures Should be as Graceful as Possible*

Perhaps it would be more accurate to state the principle negatively and say that gestures should not be *awkward*. Awkward gestures call attention to themselves; they cease to be signs and are noticed as things in themselves. Gracefulness means that the action should be both *easy* and *strong*. In gesture the curved or broken line is more graceful than the straight line. Jerky, abrupt, and angular gestures are likely to call attention to themselves and away from the meaning.

## *2. Gestures Should Precede Utterance*

We have seen that gesture as a part of general physical activity develops before voice and language. Men almost always speak first by posture, movement, and gesture; and after that by words. Watch others and see how this works. Reverse this order and you get comic and ludicrous effects. Say something with voice and words first and then add the gestures and see what happens. Tell someone, "The child was *so* tall." Wait until you have spoken the words and then indicate "*so* tall" by gesture. This will prove to be funny because you have broken the law that gesture should come before voice and words. "Ideas are conveyed largely by suggestion; not by detailed spelling out of a message but by a flash, a picture. We flash an idea across and then spell it out in words to verify it."*

*J. M. Clapp, *Talking Business*, p. 61.

101

# References

Ada, Alma Flor. 1993. *My Name Is Maria Isabel*. New York: Simon and Schuster.

———. 1993. *Me llamo Maria Isabel*. New York: Simon and Schuster.

Adams, Marilyn J. 1990. *Beginning to Read: Thinking and Learning About Print*. Cambridge, MA: MIT Press.

Adams, Marilyn J., and Maggie Bruck. 1995. "Resolving the 'Great Debate'." *American Educator* 19 (2): 7, 10–20.

Brown, Joel, Kenneth S. Goodman, and A. M. Marek. 1996. *Studies in Miscue Analysis: An Annotated Bibliography*. Newark, DE: International Reading Association.

Buswell, Guy T. 1922. *Fundamental Reading Habits: A Study of Their Development*. Chicago: University of Chicago.

Cambourne, Brian, and Yetta Goodman. 1996. "Cooperative Cloze Strategy." In *Whole Language Voices in Teacher Education*, edited by Kathryn Whitmore and Yetta Goodman, 146. York, ME: Stenhouse.

Colby, Carroll B. 1973. "Waterford Ghost's Revenge." In *The Weirdest People in the World*. New York: Sterling.

Dechant, Emerald. 1981. *Diagnosis and Remediation of Reading Disabilities*. Englewood Cliffs, NJ: Prentice-Hall.

Dewey, John, and Arthur F. Bentley. 1949. *Knowing and the Known*. Boston: Beacon Press.

Dodge, Raymond. 1900. "Visual Perceptions During Eye Movement." *Psychological Review* VII: 454–465.

Duckett, Peter. 2001. First Grade Beginning Readers' Use of Pictures and Print as They Read: A Miscue Analysis and Eye Movement Study. Unpublished doctoral dissertation, University of Arizona, Tucson, Arizona.

———. 2002. "New Insights: Eye Fixations and the Reading Process." *Talking Points* 13 (2): 16–21.

Ekwall, Eldon E. 1981. *Locating and Correcting Reading Difficulties*. 3d ed. Columbus, OH: Charles E. Merrill.

Fairbanks, Grant. 1937. "The Relation Between Eye-Movements and Voice in the Oral Reading of Good and Poor Silent Readers." *Psychological Monographs* XLVIII (3): 78–107.

Fisher, Donald F., and Wayne L. Shebilske. 1985. "There Is More That Meets the Eye Than the Eye Mind Assumption." In *Eye Movements and Human Information Processing*, edited by Rudolph Groner, George W. McConkie, and Christine Menz, 149–57. Amsterdam, Netherlands: Elsevier Science Publishers B. V.

Foglino, Annette. 1998. "Frugal Gourmets." *Civilization*. August/September. p. 30.

Fosnot, Catherine T. 1996. "Constructivism: A Psychological Theory of Learning." In *Constructivism: Theory, Perspectives, and Practice*, edited by Catherine T. Fosnot, 8–33. New York: Teacher's College, Columbia University.

Freeman, Ann. 2001. The Eyes Have It: Oral Miscue and Eye Movement Analysis of the Reading of Fourth Grade Spanish/English Bilinguals. Unpublished doctoral dissertation, University of Arizona, Tucson, Arizona.

Freeman, David E., and Yvonne S. Freeman. 2000. *Teaching Reading in Multilingual Classrooms*. Portsmouth, NH: Heinemann.

Freeman, Yvonne, Ann Freeman, and David Freeman. 2003. "Home Run Books: Connecting Students to Culturally Revelant Text." *NABE News* 26 (3): 5–8, 11–12.

Gollasch, Frederick V. 1980. Readers' Perception in Detecting and Processing Embedded Errors in Meaningful Text. Unpublished doctoral dissertation, University of Arizona, Tucson, Arizona.

Goodman, Kenneth S. 1994. "Reading, Writing, and Written Texts: A Transactional Sociopsycholinguistic View." In *Theoretical Models and Processes of Reading*, 4th ed., edited by Robert B. Ruddell, Martha Rapp Ruddell, and Harry Singer, 1093–130. Newark, DE: International Reading Association.

———. 1996. *On Reading*. Portsmouth, NH: Heinemann.

Goodman, Yetta M. 1996. "Revaluing Readers While Readers Revalue Themselves: Retrospective Miscue Analysis." *The Reading Teacher* 49 (8): 600–609.

Goodman, Yetta M., and Ann M. Marek. 1996a. *Retrospective Miscue Analysis*. Katonah, NY: Richard C. Owen.

———. 1996b. "Retrospective Miscue Analysis." In *Retrospective Miscue Analysis*, edited by Yetta M. Goodman and Ann M. Marek. Katonah, NY: Richard C. Owen.

Goodman, Yetta M., Dorothy J. Watson, and Carolyn L. Burke. 1987. *Reading Miscue Inventory*. Katonah, NY: Richard C. Owen.

————. 1996. *Reading Strategies: Focus on Comprehension*. 2d ed. Katonah, NY: Richard C. Owen.

Gough, Philip B. 1972. "One Second of Reading." In *Language by Ear and by Eye: The Relationships Between Speech and Reading*, edited by James F. Kavanagh and Ignatius G. Mattingly, 331–58. Cambridge, MA: MIT Press.

Gould, June S. 1996. "A Constructivist Perspective on Teaching and Learning in the Language Arts." In *Constructivism: Theory, Perspectives, and Practice*, edited by C. T. Fosnot, 92–102. New York: Teacher's College, Columbia University.

Grossen, Bonita. 1997. 30 Years of Research: What We Now Know About How Children Learn to Read. ERIC Document Reproduction Service Number ED415492.

Haber, Ralph Norman, and Maurice Hershenson. 1973. *The Psychology of Visual Perception*. New York: Holt, Rinehart and Winston.

Hogaboam, Thomas W. 1983. "Reading Patterns in Eye Movement Data." In *Eye Movements in Reading*, edited by Keith Rayner, 309–32. New York: Academic Press.

Huey, Edmund B. 1908. *The Psychology and Pedagogy of Reading*. Republished in 1968. Cambridge, MA: MIT Press.

Just, Marcel Adam, and Patricia A. Carpenter. 1984. "Using Eye Fixations to Study Reading Comprehension." In *New Methods in Reading Comprehension Research*, edited by David E. Kieras and Marcel Adam Just, 151–82. Hillsdale, NJ: Lawrence Erlbaum Associates.

————. 1987. *The Psychology of Reading and Language Comprehension*. Newton, MA: Allyn and Bacon.

Kant, Immanuel. 1781/1901. *Critique of Pure Reason*. Translated by John Miller Dow Meiklejohn. New York: Collier and Son.

Knowles, Malcom S., Elwood F. Holton III, and Richard A. Swanson. 1998. *The Adult Learner: The Definitive Classic in Adult Education and Human Resource Development*. 5th ed. Houston, TX: Gulf.

Liberman, Isabelle Y., and Alvin M. Liberman. 1992. "Whole Language Versus Code Emphasis: Underlying Assumptions and Their Implications for Reading Instruction." In *Reading Acquisition*, edited by Philip B. Gough, Linnea C. Ehri, and Rebecca Treiman, 343–66. Hillsdale, NJ: Lawrence Erlbaum Associates.

Mirseitova, Sapargul, and Eric J. Paulson. 2000. The Eye Movements of Russian and English Readers. National Kazakhstan Reading Conference, Almaty, Kazakhstan.

Nicholson, Tom, P. David Pearson, and R. Dykstra. 1979. "Effects of Embedded Anomalies and Oral Reading Errors on Children's Understanding of Stories." *Journal of Reading Behavior* XI (4): 339–54.

O'Regan, J. Kevin. 1979. "Moment to Moment Control of Eye Saccades as a Function of Textual Parameters in Reading." In *Processing of Visible Language*, Vol. 1, edited by Paul A. Kolers, Merald E. Wrolstad, and Herman Bouma. New York: Plenum Press.

Paulson, Eric J. 2000. Adult Readers' Eye Movements During the Production of Oral Miscues. Unpublished doctoral dissertation, University of Arizona, Tucson, Arizona.

———. 2002. "Are Oral Reading Word Omissions and Substitutions Caused by Careless Eye Movements?" *Reading Psychology* 23 (1): 45–66.

Paulson, Eric J., and Jeanne Henry. 2002. "Does the Degrees of Reading Power Assessment Reflect the Reading Process? An Eye Movement Examination." *Journal of Adolescent and Adult Literacy* 46 (3): 234–44.

Pressley, Michael. 1998. *Reading Instruction That Works*. New York: Guilford Press.

Rayner, Keith. 1995. "Eye Movements and Cognitive Processes in Reading, Visual Search, and Scene Perception." In *Eye Movement Research: Mechanisms, Processes, and Applications*, edited by John M. Findlay, Robin Walker, and Robert W. Kentridge, 3–22. New York: Elsevier.

———. 1997. "Understanding Eye Movements in Reading." *Scientific Studies of Reading* 1 (4): 317–39.

Rayner, Keith, and Alexander Pollatsek. 1989. *The Psychology of Reading*. Hillsdale, NJ: Lawrence Erlbaum Associates.

Rayner, Keith, and Sara C. Sereno. 1994. "Eye Movements in Reading: Psycholinguistic Studies." In *Handbook of Psycholinguistics* edited by M. A. Gernsbacher, 57–81. San Diego: Academic Press.

Rayner, Keith, and Arnold D. Well. 1996. "Effects of Contextual Constraint on Eye Movements in Reading: A Further Examination." *Psychonomic Bulletin and Review* 3 (4): 504–509.

Reichle, Erik D., Alexander Pollatsek, Donald L. Fisher, and Keith Rayner. 1998. "Toward a Model of Eye Movement Control in Reading." *Psychological Review* 105 (1): 125–57.

Rekrut, Martha D. 1995. "Review of *Reading and Learning in Content Areas* by Randall J. Ryder and Michael F. Graves." *Journal of Reading* 38 (5): 412–14.

Rosenblatt, Louise M. 1978. *The Reader, the Text, the Poem: the Transactional Theory of the Literary Work*. Carbondale, IL: Southern Illinois University Press.

Rumelhart, David E. 1994. "Toward an Interactive Model of Reading." In *Theoretical Models and Processes of Reading*, 4th ed., edited by Robert B. Ruddell, Martha Rapp Ruddell, and Harry Singer, 864–94. Newark, DE: International Reading Association.

Singer, Peter. 1983. "Hegel." In *German Philosophers: Kant, Hegel, Schopenhauer, Nietzsche*, 1997, edited by K. Thomas, 105–214. Oxford: Oxford University Press.

Smith, Frank. 1994. *Understanding Reading: A Psycholinguistic Analysis of Reading and Learning to Read*. 5th ed. Hillsdale, NJ: Lawrence Erlbaum Associates.

Sotiriou, Peter E. 2002. *Integrating College Study Skills*. 6th ed. Belmont, CA: Wadsworth.

Sun, Fuchuan, Michon Morita, and Lawrence W. Stark. 1985. "Comparative Patterns of Reading Eye Movement in Chinese and English." *Perception and Psychophysics* 37 (6): 502–506.

Taylor, Insup, and M. Martin Taylor. 1983. *The Psychology of Reading*. New York: Academic Press.

Underwood, Geoffrey, and Vivienne Batt. 1996. *Reading and Understanding*. Oxford: Blackwell Publishers.

Vadeboncoeur, Jennifer A. 1997. "Child Development and the Purpose of Education: A Historical Context for Constructivism in Teacher Education." In *Constructivist Teacher Education: Building a World of New Understandings*, edited by Virginia Richardson, 15–37. London: Falmer Press.

Van Der Kamp, Max. 1992. "Effective Adult Learning." In *Learning Across the Lifespan: Theories, Research, Policies*, edited by Albert C. Tuijnman and Max Van Der Kamp, 191–203. Oxford: Pergamon Press.

Viorst, Judith. 1972. *Alexander and the Terrible, Horrible, No Good, Very Bad Day*. New York: Atheneum.

Wilde, Sandra. 2000. *Miscue Analysis Made Easy: Building on Student Strengths*. Portsmouth, NH: Heinemann.

Wolverton, Gary S., and David Zola. 1983. "The Temporal Characteristics of Visual Information Extraction During Reading." In *Eye Movements in Reading: Perceptual and Language Processes*, edited by K. Rayner, 41–51. New York: Academic Press.

Woobert, Charles Henry, and Andrew Thomas Weaver. 1922. *Better Speech: A Textbook of Speech Training for Secondary Schools*. New York: Harcourt, Brace and Company.

Xu, Jinguo. 1998. A Study of the Reading Process in Chinese Through Detecting Errors in a Meaningful Text. Unpublished doctoral dissertation, University of Arizona, Tucson, Arizona.

# Index